IN PRAISE OF THE

COGNITIVE

EMOTIONS

IN PRAISE OF THE

COGNITIVE

EMOTIONS

AND OTHER ESSAYS IN THE PHILOSOPHY OF EDUCATION

ISRAEL SCHEFFLER

ROUTLEDGE
NEW YORK • LONDON

First published in 1991 by

Routledge
an imprint of
Routledge, Chapman & Hall, Inc.
29 West 35 Street
New York, NY 10001

Published in Great Britain by

Routledge
11 New Fetter Lane
London EC4P 4EE

Library of Congress Cataloging in Publication Data

Scheffler, Israel.
   In praise of the cognitive emotions and other essays in the
philosophy of education / Israel Scheffler.
     p. cm.
   Collection of articles spanning 1974 to 1990.
   Includes bibliographical references and index.
   ISBN 0-415-90363-7   ISBN 0-415-90364-5 (pbk.)
   1. Education—Philosophy. 2. Emotions and cognition. 3. Critical
thinking—Study and teaching. I. Title.
   LB885.S34I5 1991
370'.1—dc20
                                90-39221

British Library cataloguing in publication data also is available

For Gabriel Alexander Scheffler

Contents

Introduction

Education is at once the most intimate and the most far-reaching of human endeavors. Through education we recall the words of our parents and touch the hearts and minds of our children. Through education we interpret nature, build civilizations, and construct the worlds of art, science, and culture. Education deserves our closest attention and most sustained reflection. It merits the best efforts of thought we can supply.

Philosophy brings to education its characteristic emphases upon clarity, purpose, and warrant. It challenges us to be clearer in our thinking, more responsible in our beliefs, and more alive to the aims and consequences of our actions. The essays in this book result from my efforts in recent years to apply philosophical thinking to various educational themes.

With the exception of one early selection, included here to round out my treatment of symbolism, the papers collected in this volume span seventeen years, all these papers having been written during the 1970s and 1980s. The book as a whole is perhaps best conceived as a sequel to *Reason and Teaching*, my last collection of papers devoted exclusively to philosophy of education. The present work picks up where that one left off, in 1971, and continues until 1990, the date of the latest paper included herein. Continuous with *Reason and Teaching* in fundamental approach, the present book nevertheless stands completely on its own.

The basis of the earlier book was "the conviction that critical thought is of the first importance in the conception and organization of educational activities."[1] That conviction continues to guide the treatment of issues in the present volume. I remain convinced that "the ideal of rationality [provides] a unifying perspective relating theory and practice, moral and intellectual schooling, general studies and teacher education, the continuity and scope of the human heritage and the independent judgment and fresh vision which constitute our best hope for the future."[2]

I have also persisted in my effort to wed an analytical style of thought to a concern with practical issues. However, I take the practical to comprehend not only the detailed urgencies of decision but also the general predispositions to behavior sanctioned by our philosophical preferences. As such, the domain of the practical embraces those ideals of learning that help to shape our educational efforts.

In previous writings, I have defended the ideal of rationality as "providing a unifying . . . focus for education, . . . tempering the extremes of formalism and preserving what is most precious in the humanistic and progressive tradition."[3] Early and late, I have insisted that rationality not be identified with a special faculty of mind called Reason, nor construed as a rule-governed mechanism of inference. Rather, I have taken it as the capacity to grasp principles and purposes, and to evaluate them in the light of reasons that might be put forward for and against them.

Further, I have connected rationality not only with the *capacity* to evaluate principles and purposes in the light of reasons, but also with the *right* to conduct such evaluation—with the autonomy of the student seeking "reasons in support of claims upon his credibilities and loyalties and [acknowledging] his correlative obligation to deal with such reasons in a principled manner."[4] There is no intent, in such interpretation, to oppose reason to the emotions, nor to identify it with the process of making logical deductions. Taking rationality as an educational ideal, I have argued, means rather making as pervasive as possible the free and critical quest for reasons in all realms of study and conduct.

These ideas, I believe, bear underscoring and elaboration in our present circumstances. For the past two decades have seen a remarkable burst of technological energy that has already transformed, and will continue to transform, a wide variety of human activities, including education. The computer is a basic vehicle of such transformation, and technical concepts of information and algorithm are its intellectual underpinnings. Opportunities for increased efficiency and individualization of learning are but two promises of the new technology that prudent educators will need to explore. But the basic hazard they will need to confront, in their fascination with developing techniques, is a narrowing of their philosophical vision—a reduction of their fundamental concepts to presumed technological correlates. It is in overcoming this hazard by promoting a broad interpretation of such concepts that philosophy may now serve education as a valuable resource.

Several selections included here elaborate this broad interpretation of the concept of rationality. The essays in Part I provide a background in human nature for the function of critical aspects of mind. Reason, viewed as an outgrowth of symbolic capacity, is portrayed in its close connections with emotion, surprise being singled out for special notice as a "cognitive emotion" of epistemological weight. Thinking is, moreover, described in its teleological and productive roles, as directed toward making as well as toward understanding. Mind is viewed in its potentialities for shaping the future as well as in its actualities at given times.

The symbolic capacities are further studied in Part II with special reference to metaphor, which is seen not as mere literary adornment or distraction but as an instrument of inquiry and a potential vehicle of truth. Analogously, ritual is analyzed as a pervasive cognitive device of symbolism rather than as a piece of archaic superstition or magic.

Part III offers a direct discussion of computer technology as applied to schooling; it urges the use of educational criteria in guiding such application and offers a critique of information models of the mind. The notion of strategic rationality is developed in the effort to gain an adequate understanding of mathematical understanding. The final essay offers a conception of moral education connecting reason with care rather than dividing the two, and emphasizing the importance of factual knowledge along with formal principle.

Part IV stresses the need for policy-makers to have not merely technical knowledge but also a grasp of the human problems naturally expressed by clients of policy. It also argues for the importance of historical sensitivity in the policy-maker's role as well as an awareness of the moral space created by policy decisions. The final paper attempts to break up the fossilized conceptions of education embodied in popular notions of educational vice and, by turning these notions on their heads, to explore the possibilities of a more flexible educational attitude.

Finally, Part V offers critical commentary on two of pragmatism's founding fathers, Charles Sanders Peirce and John Dewey. In each of the two essays in this part, I have striven to come to grips with the key ideas of the author in question, offering not only a critique but also a sympathetic view of elements I have found persuasive in my own thinking on major philosophical topics and on educational practice.

The selections comprising this volume are connected in various ways with others of my books. A general account of the work of the early pragmatists—including, in addition to Peirce and Dewey, William James and George Herbert Mead—is given in my *Four Pragmatists*.[5] The second selection of Part I and the first selection of Part IV are precursors of chapters in my *Of Human Potential*,[6] which develops their themes more fully. The epistemological views of the title essay of this book are elaborations of ideas I set forth earlier, in *Science and Subjectivity*.[7] More general aspects of my approach to epistemological topics are to be found in my still earlier *Anatomy of Inquiry*[8] and *Conditions of Knowledge*,[9] as well as in *Inquiries*.[10] The discussion of metaphor in Part II is closely related to my *Beyond the Letter*,[11] and the discussion of ritual in the same part draws upon my treatment of this subject in *Inquiries*. While these other books will provide a significantly deeper understanding of my views, none of the books in question is a prerequisite for this one, which will in fact serve as a useful introduction to my work in educational philosophy.

I am grateful to all those publishers who gave permission to reprint. Specific acknowledgments are made in footnotes to the selections themselves. I thank Harvey Siegel, who kindly offered comments on the collection as a whole. And I am grateful to JoAnne Sorabella, who helped in every phase of the preparation of the manuscript.

Notes

1. Israel Scheffler, *Reason and Teaching* (Indianapolis, Ind.: Hackett Publishing Co., 1973), p. 1.

2. Ibid.

3. I. Scheffler, "Concepts of Education: Reflections on the Current Scene," in ibid., p. 63.

4. Ibid., p. 78.

5. I. Scheffler, *Four Pragmatists* (London: Routledge, 1974).

6. I. Scheffler, *Of Human Potential* (London: Routledge, 1985).

7. I. Scheffler, *Science and Subjectivity* (Indianapolis, Ind.: Hackett Publishing Co., 1967).

8. I. Scheffler, *The Anatomy of Inquiry* (New York: Alfred A. Knopf, 1963).

9. I. Scheffler, *Conditions of Knowledge* (Chicago: University of Chicago Press, 1965).

10. I. Scheffler, *Inquiries* (Indianapolis, Ind., Hackett Publishing Company, 1986).

11. I. Scheffler, *Beyond the Letter* (London: Routledge, 1979).

Part I

Human Nature

1

In Praise of the
Cognitive Emotions

The mention of cognitive emotions may well evoke emotions of perplexity or incredulity. For cognition and emotion, as everyone knows, are hostile worlds apart. Cognition is sober inspection; it is the scientist's calm apprehension of fact after fact in his relentless pursuit of Truth. Emotion, on the other hand, is commotion—an unruly inner turbulence fatal to such pursuit but finding its own constructive outlets in aesthetic experience and moral or religious commitment.

Strongly entrenched, this opposition of cognition and emotion must nevertheless be challenged, for it distorts everything it touches: mechanizing science, it sentimentalizes art, while portraying ethics and religion as twin swamps of feeling and unreasoned commitment. Education, meanwhile—that is to say, the development of mind and attitudes in the young—is split into two grotesque parts: unfeeling knowledge and mindless arousal. My purpose here is to help overcome the breach by outlining basic aspects of emotion in the cognitive process.

Some misgivings about this purpose will, I hope, be allayed by a preliminary word. My aim, to begin with, is not reductive; I am concerned neither to reduce emotion to cognition nor cognition to emotion, only to show how cognitive functioning employs and incorporates diverse emotional elements—these elements themselves acquiring cognitive significance thereby. I am emphatically not suggesting that cognitions are essentially emotions, or that emotions are, in reality, only cognitions. Nevertheless, I hold that cognition cannot be cleanly sundered from emotion and assigned to science, while emotion is ceded to the arts, ethics, and religion. All these spheres of life involve both fact and feeling; they relate to sense as well as sensibility.

Second, though applauding the cognitive import of emotions, I do not propose to surrender intellectual controls to wishful thinking, nor shall I portray the heart as giving special access to a higher truth.[1] Control of

---

Presented as a special lecture in May 1976 at the 129th annual meeting of the American Psychiatric Association. Published in *Teachers College Record*, 79, no. 2 (1977): 171–86.

3

wishful thinking is utterly essential in cognition; it operates, however, not through an unfeeling faculty of Reason but through the organization of countervailing critical interests in the process of inquiry. These interests of a critical intellect are, in principle, no less emotive in their bearing than those of wayward wish. The heart, in sum, provides no substitute for critical inquiry; it beats in the service of science as well as of private desire.

Finally, I concede it to be undeniable that certain emotional states may be at odds with sound processes of judgment and decision making. Overpowering agitations may derail the course of reasoning; greed, jealousy, or lust may misdirect it; depression or terror may bring it to a total halt. Conversely, the effect of rational judgment may well be to moderate, even wholly to dissipate, certain emotions by falsifying their factual presuppositions: anger fades, for example, when it turns out the injury was accidental or caused by someone other than first supposed; fear evaporates when the menacing figure becomes the tree's dancing shadow. It does not follow from these cases, however, that *emotion* as such is uniformly hostile to cognitive endeavors, nor may we properly conclude that *cognition* is, in general, free of emotional engagement. Indeed, emotion without cognition is blind, and, as I shall hope particularly to show in the sequel, cognition without emotion is vacuous.

Emotions in the Service of Cognition

Considering now the various roles of emotion in cognition, I divide the field, for convenience, into two main parts, the first having to do with the organization of *emotions generally* in the service of critical inquiry, and the second having to do with *specifically cognitive emotions*. Under the first rubric I shall treat: (a) rational passions,[2] (b) perceptive feelings, and (c) theoretical imagination. I turn first to the rational passions, that is to say, to the emotions undergirding the life of reason.

Rational Passions

The life of reason is one in which cognitive processes are organized in accord with controlling rational ideals and norms. Such organization involves characteristic patterns of thought, action, and evaluation comprising what may be called rational character. Thus it also requires suitable emotional dispositions. It demands, for example, a love of truth and a contempt for lying, a concern for accuracy in observation and inference, and a corresponding repugnance at error in logic or fact. It demands revulsion at distortion, disgust at evasion, admiration of theoretical achievement, respect for the considered arguments of others. Failing such demands, we incur rational shame; fulfilling them makes for rational self-respect.

Like moral character, rational character requires that the right acts and judgments be habitual; it also requires that the right emotions be attached to the right acts and judgments.[3] "A rational man," says R. S. Peters, "cannot, without some special explanation, slap his sides and roar with laughter or shrug his shoulders with indifference if he is told that what he says is irrelevant, that his thinking is confused and inconsistent or that it flies in the face of the evidence."[4] The suitable deployment in conduct of emotional dispositions such as love and hate, contempt and disgust, shame and self-esteem, respect and admiration indeed defines what is meant, quite generally, by the internalization of ideals and principles in character. The wonder is not that *rational* character is thus related to the emotions but that anyone should ever have supposed it to be an exception to the general rule.

Rational character constitutes an intellectual conscience; it monitors and curbs evasions and distortions; it combats inconsistency, unfairness to the facts, and wishful thinking. In thus exercising control over undesirable impulses, it works for a balance in thought, an epistemic justice, which requires its own special renunciations and develops a characteristic cognitive discipline. There is, however, no question here of the control of impulses through a "bloodless reason,"[5] as control is exercised through the structuring of emotions themselves. Rationality, as John Dewey put it,

> is not a force to evoke against impulse and habit. It is the attainment of a working harmony among diverse desires. . . . The elaborate systems of science are born not of reason but of impulses at first slight and flickering; impulses to handle, move about, to hunt, to uncover, to mix things separated and divide things combined, to talk and to listen. Method is their effectual organization into continuous dispositions of inquiry, development and testing. It occurs after these acts and because of their consequences. Reason, the rational attitude, is the resulting disposition. . . . The man who would intelligently cultivate intelligence will widen, not narrow, his life of strong impulses while aiming at their happy coincidence in operation.[6]

This coincidence, I emphasize, requires appropriate organization of feelings and sentiments in the interests of intelligent control.

Perceptive Feelings

Having seen the role of emotions in the internalization of rational norms, let us consider now their employment in perception. For they are not only interwoven with our cognitive ideals and evaluative principles; they are also intimately tied to our vision of the external world. Indeed, they help to construct that vision and to define the critical features of that world.

These critical features—however specified—are the objects of our evaluative attitudes, the foci of our appraisals of the environment. Our habits and judgments are keyed in to these appraisals; we define ourselves and orient our actions in the light of our situation as appraised. Characteristic orientations are associated with distinctive emotional dispositions, and both involve seeing the environment in a certain light: is it, for example, beneficial or harmful, promising or threatening, fulfilling or thwarting?[7] The subtle and intricate web relating adult feeling and orientation to adult perception of the environment is a product of evolutionary development, to be sure, but also of the special circumstances of individual biography. Acquiring human significance through biographical linkage with critical features of the environment, our feelings come indeed to *signify*—to serve as available cues for interpreting the situation.

Fear of a particular person, for example, presupposes that that person is regarded as dangerous—danger being a critical feature of the environment calling for a special orientation in response. There need, however, be no *independent* evidence, in every case, of the threat we sense: the characteristic feeling that has become associated for us with past dangers itself serves us as a cue. Interpreting that feeling *as* fear, we at once characterize our own state and ascribe danger to the environment. Indeed, we may thence proceed to an explicit attribution of danger, prompted by cues of feeling. Pursuing a more abstract direction in forming our cognitive concepts, we may, further, come to describe a certain situation as *terrifying,* ascribing to it, *independently of our own state,* the capacity to arouse fear. Thus employing the emotions as parameters, we gain enormous new powers of fundamental description, while abstracting from actual conditions of feeling.

The notion that aesthetic experience, for example, is peculiarly and purely a matter of emotion ignores such manifold connections of feeling and fact— both fact as *embodied* in the art work and fact as *represented* therein. Relative to the latter, H. D. Aiken writes:

> Just as in ordinary circumstances an emotional response is the product of a perceived situation which is apprehended by the individual as promising or threatening, so the expressiveness of an imaginative work arises, at least in part, from the fact that it provides a dramatic representation of an action of which the evoked emotion is the expressive counterpart. And such a representation must be understood as such if the expressive values of the work are to become actual; without it such emotion as the observer might experience would have no ground, and if, by a miracle, it could be sustained, it would still remain the private, dumb, inexpressive importation of the observer himself. As such it would be nothing more than an accidental, adventitious subjective coloring which, having no artistic basis in the thing perceived, would be devoid of aesthetic relevance to it. Aesthetically relevant emotion in art is something which is expressed to us by the action

or gesture of the work itself; it is something aroused and sustained by the work as an object for contemplation, and it is found there as a projected quality of the action.[8]

That emotion is thus tied to a representational understanding of the work of art does not imply, however, that this understanding must be antecedently fashioned, in complete isolation from the feelings. This point must be especially emphasized because the familiar notion of the work of art as "an object for contemplation" may carry contrary, and therefore misleading, connotations. In fact, I believe, the very feelings through which we respond to the content of a work serve us also in interpreting this content. Reading our feelings and reading the work are, in general, virtually inseparable processes.

The cognitive role of the emotions in aesthetic contexts has been emphasized by Nelson Goodman in a recent discussion. He writes:

> The work of art is apprehended through the feelings as well as through the senses. Emotional numbness disables here as definitely if not as completely as blindness or deafness. Nor are the feelings used exclusively for exploring the emotional content of a work. To some extent, we may feel how a painting looks as we may see how it feels. The actor or dancer—or the spectator—sometimes notes and remembers the feeling of a movement rather than its pattern, insofar as the two can be distinguished at all. Emotion in aesthetic experience is a means of discerning what properties a work has and expresses.[9]

The general point is, of course, not limited to the aesthetic realm for, as I have emphasized earlier, the emotions intimately mesh with all critical appraisals of the environment: the flow of feeling thus provides us with a continuous stream of cues significant for orientation to our changing contexts. Indeed, as Goodman remarks:

> In daily life, classification of things by feeling is often more vital than classification by other properties: we are likely to be better off if we are skilled in fearing, wanting, braving, or distrusting the right things, animate or inanimate, than if we perceive only their shapes, sizes, weights, etc. And the importance of discernment by feeling does not vanish when the motivation becomes theoretic rather than practical. . . . Indeed, in any science, while the requisite objectivity forbids wishful thinking, prejudicial reading of evidence, rejection of unwanted results, avoidance of ominous lines of inquiry, it does not forbid use of feeling in exploration and discovery, the impetus of inspiration and curiosity, or the cues given by excitement over intriguing problems and promising hypotheses.[10]

Theoretical Imagination

Mention of the context of theory brings us to the third role of emotions in the service of cognition, that of stimulus to the scientific imagination. This role is virtually annihilated by the stereotyped emotion-cognition dichotomy. For this dichotomy assigns all feeling and flair, all fantasy and fun, to the arts and humanities, conceiving the sciences as grim and humorless grind. The method of science is miserly caution—to gather the facts and guard the hoard. Imagination is a seductive distraction—a hindrance to serious scientific business.

This doctrine is, in fact, the death of theory. Theory is not reducible to mere fact-gathering, and theoretical creation is beyond the reach of any mechanical routine. Science controls theory by credibility, logic, and simplicity; it does not provide rules for the creation of theoretical ideas. Scientific objectivity demands allegiance to fair controls over theory, but fair controls cannot substitute for ideas. "All our thinking," said Albert Einstein, "is of this nature of a free play with concepts, the justification for this play lying in the measure of survey over the experience of the senses which we are able to achieve with its aid."[11]

The ideal theorist, loyal to the demands of rational character and the institutions of scientific objectivity, is not therefore passionless and prim. Theoretical inventiveness requires not caution but boldness, verve, speculative daring. Imagination is no hindrance but the very life of theory, without which there *is* no science.

Now the emotions relate to imaginative theorizing in a variety of ways. The emotional life, to begin with, is a rich source of substantive ideas. Drawing from the obscure wellsprings of this life, the mind's free play casts up novel patterns and images, exotic figures and analogies that, in an investigative context, may serve to place old facts in a new light. The dream of the nineteenth-century chemist F. A. Kekulé will provide a striking illustration. He had been trying for a long time to find a structural formula for the benzene molecule. Dozing in front of his fireplace one evening in 1865, he seemed, as he looked into the flames, "to see atoms dancing in snakelike arrays. Suddenly, one of the snakes formed a ring by seizing hold of its own tail and then whirled mockingly before him. Kekulé awoke in a flash: he had hit upon the now famous and familiar idea of representing the molecular structure of benzene by a hexagonal ring. He spent the rest of the night working out the consequences of this hypothesis."[12]

The emotions serve not merely as a *source* of imaginative patterns; they fulfill also a *selective* function, facilitating choice among these patterns, defining their salient features, focusing attention accordingly. The patterns developed in imagination, that is, carry their own emotive values; these values guide selection and emphasis. They help imagined patterns to structure the phenomena, highlighting factual features of interest to further inquiry. "Passions," as Michael Polanyi has said, "charge objects with emotions, making them repulsive or attractive; . . . Only a tiny fraction of all knowable facts are of interest to scientists, and scientific passion serves . . . as a guide in the assessment of what is of higher and what of lesser interest."[13]

Finally, the emotions play a directive role in the process of *applying* the fruits of imagination to the solution of problems. The course of problem-solving, as has already been intimated, is continually monitored by the theorist's cues of feeling, his sense of excitement or anticipation, his elation or suspicion or gloom. Moreover, imagined objects encountered in thought by the problem-solver affect his deliberation emotively, as real objects do, and influence his decisions in analogous ways. "In thought as well as in overt action," says Dewey, "the objects experienced in following out a course of action attract, repel, satisfy, annoy, promote and retard. Thus deliberation proceeds."[14] There is, no doubt, much yet to be learned about the interaction of emotions and imagination in all the ways I have sketched, and in others as well. It should, however, even now, be evident that creation is fed by the emotional life in the sphere of science no less than in the spheres of poetry and the arts.

Cognitive Emotions

We have, until now, concerned ourselves with the organization of emotions generally in the service of cognition. I want now to deal with two emotions that are, in a sense to be explained, *specifically cognitive* in their bearing—the *joy of verification* and the *feeling of surprise*.

In what sense do I speak of an emotion as specifically cognitive? Consider first the notion of *moral emotions,* conceived as those resting upon suppositions of a moral sort: Thus indignation, for example, rests upon the supposition of a moral grievance—a piece of injustice—and remorse presumes that one has in fact done something wrong. If the relevant moral suppositions are false or lack evidential foundation, the respective emotions may be thought unreasonable, but if these suppositions are not made at all, that is to say, if the suppositions do not exist, the emotions in question can hardly, in normal circumstances, be said to have occurred. Now I propose, analogously, to consider an emotion specifically *cognitive* if it rests upon a supposition of a cognitive sort—that is to say, a supposition relating to the content of the subject's cognitions (beliefs, predictions, expectations) and, in cases of special interest to us, bearing upon their epistemological status.

It is important to avoid misunderstanding the terminology I have chosen here. It is indeed true that *all* suppositions may be considered cognitive in a broad sense, inasmuch as they make factual claims expressible in propositional form; moreover, emotions *generally,* as I have maintained, presuppose the existence of such claims concerning critical features of the environment. However, when I characterize an emotion as *specifically cognitive,* I mean more than this. In particular, I mean not simply that it presupposes the existence of a factual claim but that the claim in question specifically concerns the nature of the subject's cognitions (and, in cases of interest, is epistemologically relevant to them). A cognitive emotion, I should further emphasize, is thus decidedly an *emotion,* but an emotion of a certain *kind,* specifiable by its cognitive reference as just explained.[15]

The Joy of Verification

In his well-known paper of 1934 on "The Foundation of Knowledge,"[16] Moritz Schlick provides an example of such a cognitive emotion in outlining his theory of science, giving primary place in his theory to the joy that accompanies the fulfillment of an expectation. Cognition, in Schlick's view, has, from the earliest times, always been predictive, but the value of reliable prediction lay originally in its practical service to life. "Now in science," he writes, "cognition . . . is not sought because of its utility. With the confirmation of prediction the scientific goal is achieved: the joy in cognition is the joy of verification, the triumphant feeling of having guessed correctly."[17] Such moments of joy are, in Schlick's opinion, of central importance in understanding scientific purpose. "They do not in any way," he says, "lie at the base of science; but like a flame, cognition, as it were, licks out to them, reaching each but for a moment and then at once consuming it. And newly fed and strengthened, it flames onward to the next. These moments of fulfillment and combustion are what is essential. All the light of knowledge comes from them."[18]

Now one need not agree with Schlick's general view of science in order to acknowledge that the satisfaction of a theoretical forecast may indeed occasion joy. Nor is it required that we concur with the extravagant suggestion that *all* predictive success brings elation. It may, for example, be countered that routine successes based on theory frequently, perhaps typically, go unnoticed, while soberly predicted events may be so dreadful as to occasion not joy but sorrow or despair. Nevertheless, we can agree that the fulfillment of a prediction may indeed crown an investigative achievement in science, producing in its wake what Schlick calls a "triumphant feeling of having guessed correctly."

This joyful feeling I consider a cognitive emotion, because it rests on a supposition (with epistemological relevance) as to the content of the guess in question: it presumes that what has happened is what had, in fact, been predicted. Without such presumption, this joy of verification cannot be said to occur. Whether the presumption is true, or is based on adequate grounds, is another story. Certainly one assumes that the emotion in question may be criticized as unreasonable if it can be shown that what has in fact happened had not, in fact, been predicted.

Can such a criticism, however, actually be entertained as a matter of psychological fact? Is it not, rather, true that our expectations are so powerful as consistently to warp our observations to fit? A whole library of psychological writings testifies to the powerful tendency of expectation to create its own confirmations in experience. The general theme of this testimony may be indicated by the role of normal cues in perception: the perceptual identification of objects "proceeds on the basis of cues normally sufficient to select the objects in question; when these cues fail in fact, we tend anyway to see them as having succeeded."[19] Bruner, Goodnow, and Austin comment on this point as follows:

> If [a bird] has wings and feathers, the bill and legs are highly predictable. In coding or categorizing the environment, one builds up an expectancy of all of these features being present together. It is this unitary conception that has the configurational or Gestalt property of "birdness." Indeed, once a configuration has been established and the object is being identified in terms of configurational attributes, the perceiver will tend to "rectify" or "normalize" any of the original defining attributes that deviate from expectancy. Missing attributes are "filled in" . . . , reversals righted . . . , colors assimilated to expectancy.[20]

Some philosophers have further maintained that scientific observation itself is *systematically* theory-laden—presupposing the very theories it is naively thought to test.[21] If indeed we are, as suggested, so blinded by our own theoretical beliefs as to be incapable of acknowledging anything that might contradict them, we can hardly take the joy of verification to represent a cognitive triumph of science. Rather, we must count it an unearned and deluded joy, resulting not from a happy match between theory and experience but solely from our desperate rigging of experience to make it fit.

This conclusion, as I have elsewhere argued, seems to me too extreme for the facts.[22] It is undeniable that our beliefs greatly influence our perceptions, but neither psychology nor philosophy offers any proof of a pre-established harmony between what we believe and what we see. Expectations have the function of orienting us selectively toward the future, but this function does not require that they blind us to the unforeseen. Indeed, the presumption of mismatch between experience and expectation underlies another cognitive emotion: *surprise*. The existence of this emotion testifies that we are not, in principle, beyond acknowledging the predictive failures of our own theories, that we are not debarred by nature from capitalizing upon such failures in order to learn from experience. The genius of science is, in fact, to institutionalize such learning by wedding the free theoretical imagination to the rigorous probing for predictive failures.

The Significance of Surprise

Surprise is a cognitive emotion, resting on the (epistemologically relevant) supposition that what has happened conflicts with prior expectation. Without such presumption, surprise cannot be supposed to occur, although the truth of the presumption may, of course, be questioned in particular cases. Surprise must, in any event, not be confused with mere novelty. A novel— that is to say, a hitherto unencountered—contingency may well be anticipated in thought, while a familiar phenomenon, juxtaposed with available theory, may profoundly surprise. Thwarting expectation, the surprising element may indeed provoke the revision of theory, even the reorganization of categories, thus *producing* novelty as a result. It is itself, however, never a mere matter of novelty, but always one of conflict with prior belief. The concept of *unexpectedness,* it should be noted, is too weak to make this critical distinction, for it covers both the case of a feature that has simply not been anticipated, and that of a feature that has been positively ruled out by anticipation.[23]

To the extent that we are capable of surprise, the possibility that our expectations are wrong is alive for us, and thus our joy in verification, if it occurs, is not utterly deluded. Receptive to surprise, we are capable of learning from experience—capable, that is, of acknowledging the inadequacies of our initial beliefs and recognizing the need for their improvement. It is thus that the testing of theories, no less than their generation, calls upon appropriate emotional dispositions.

Receptivity to surprise involves, however, a certain vulnerability; it means accepting the risk of a possibly painful unsettlement of one's beliefs, with the attendant need to rework one's expectations and redirect one's conduct. To be sure, where the relevant beliefs are weakly held, or relatively segregated, or of peripheral significance for one's basic orientation—or where the required alterations are likely to be readily effected—the risk may be easily borne, even by the cautious. Surprise may, in such circumstances, not in fact distress but amuse—even enchant, as will be evident from even brief reflection on the role of surprise in humor, in music, in literature, and generally in the arts. Moreover, there are, in all realms of life, pleasant surprises, where the value of the surprising event, or even of the unsettlement itself, outweighs the stress of disorientation and the concomitant costs of revision in belief.

One cannot, however, reasonably count on all—even most—surprises in life to be thus amusing or pleasant; it must be conceded that a general openness to surprise involves a real risk of epistemic distress. This risk may to varying degrees become palatable, even exciting; certainly, accepting it is one of the normal requirements of rational character. Yet it *is* a risk of possibly painful disorientation, and it requires emotional strength to face and to master. To commit oneself to learning from experience is, in short, a significant attitude—supported by mature reflection, to be sure—but exacting a price in return for the prospect of improvement in one's system of beliefs.

Three alternative attitudes promise an avoidance of the price by erecting wholesale defenses against surprise. Because surprise presumes prior expectation, a defense may be sought, to begin with, in the *rejection* of all expectation—in effect, in the denial of all belief. This is the attitude of the radical skeptic, who hopes to make himself immune to surprise by any contingency through renouncing all anticipations to the contrary, that is to say, all anticipations without exception. Of whatever happens, he says, in effect, "It doesn't surprise me since I never expected it not to happen!" A second—apparently opposite—attitude is that of utter credulity or gullibility: the *acceptance* of all beliefs or expectations without distinction. Here the formula in response to every contingency is "I'm not surprised! I expected that too!" Both radical skepticism and radical credulity are, however, forms of epistemic apathy: to reject all expectations is to be indifferent to each, while to accept all as equally good is in actuality to choose none, having no reason to expect anything at all rather than something else. It is no wonder that these seemingly contrary attitudes have so often been remarked to be psychologically akin, and together opposed to the selective hypothesis-formation characteristic of scientific thought. "Complete doubt," as Peirce noted, is "a mere self-deception," and no one who follows the method of radical skepticism "will ever be satisfied until he has formally recovered all those beliefs which in form he has given up."[24]

Moreover, each of these two alternative attitudes exacts its own heavy price. Neither can in fact be realized as a genuine option over a significant area of conduct. The skeptic, despite himself, forms positive expectations in executing his actions, while the radically credulous person, generally hospitable to inconsistencies, perforce rules out certain contingencies in carrying through the activities of daily life. Only in a local and intermittent way can these attitudes be attempted. They are perhaps more accurately described as poses or pretenses, the effect of which is, however, perfectly real—to aid the denial of responsibility for one's beliefs and so to block the possibility of their improvement through the educative medium of surprise.

The third attitude promising a defense against surprise is that of dogmatism. Unlike the radical skeptic and the total believer, the dogmatist is perfectly firm about the beliefs he espouses and the beliefs he rejects. He blocks surprise not by disclaiming responsibility for his doctrines, but rather by denying all experience that purports to contradict them. He not only avoids the systematic testing of his beliefs; he closes off the very possibility of recognizing negative evidence, by early and stout denial of its existence. Theory-laden to the point of blindness, his observations are predictably positive, the joy he takes in verification thus unearned and hollow. Dogmatism is also a difficult attitude to maintain, if only because (as Peirce saw)[25] it is impossible to filter out all negative indications in advance by a systematic method. Yet it can be carried a long way, preventing the acknowledgment of surprise and, hence, the application of new and surprising experience to the improvement of initial beliefs and orientations. Dogmatism, no less than skepticism and gullibility, conflicts with the effort at such improvement. To accept this effort, with its associated vulnerability to the unsettlement of surprise, is to choose a distinctive emotional, as well as cognitive, path.

But how, it may be asked, is receptivity to surprise possible? Surprise is, after all, unsettling; it risks the distress of disorientation and the potential pain of relearning. In similar vein, Schlick contrasts the joy of verification with the disappointment of falsification[26]—the disappointment following upon the violation of beliefs in which we had put our trust. How can one counsel receptivity to surprise: is this not an impossibly mixed emotion, like elation at despair, or happiness at depression?

We must, first of all, reject the suggestion that surprise is always painful. If Schlick's notion of uniformly joyful verification is to be rejected as extravagant, in line with our earlier remarks, his parallel notion of uniformly disappointing falsification must equally be criticized. Some falsifications are, as we have previously intimated, delightful, some disruptions of expectation pleasantly exciting, some occasions of relearning fraught with engaging challenge. Schlick, I suggest, confuses expectation with hope, but the two are clearly separable, and only the former is necessary for surprise.

Yet if surprise is not always painful, surely it sometimes is: it must therefore be conceded, at the very least, to be *uncertain* in its quality. The question then recurs in a new version: How can one counsel receptivity to uncertainty? Here, however, an immediate reply is forthcoming. The original version of the question raised the issue of impossibly mixed emotions, whereas the present version no longer does so. For uncertainty is not an emotion; it is rather a prospect or condition, while the *feeling* of uncertainty mixes readily with receptive and aversive attitudes. Uncertainty is indeed consistently faced in varying ways: some persons tend to shrink from, while others tend to welcome, the prospect. The receptivity to surprise that is implicated in the capacity to learn from experience is, in any case, perfectly coherent in its emotional composition.

Moreover, *receptivity* to surprise is not to be confused with elation or happiness. It is rather the capability of acknowledging surprise than joy in its occurrence that is here in point. Analogously, to acknowledge one's grief does not entail being elated by it. Acknowledgment itself is a possible and a significant attitude, opening the way beyond the acknowledged circumstance.

Yet receptivity is, of course, not enough to characterize the testing phase of inquiry. How we cope with surprise, once it is acknowledged, is of critical importance. Surprise may be dissipated and may evaporate into lethargy. It may culminate in confusion or panic. It may be swiftly overcome by a redoubled dogmatism. Or it may be transformed into wonder or curiosity, and so become an educative occasion. Curiosity replaces the impact of surprise with the demand for explanation[27]; it turns confusion into question. To answer the question is to reconstruct initial beliefs so that they may consistently incorporate what had earlier been unassimilable. It is to provide an improved framework of premises by which the surprising event might have been anticipated and for which parallel events will no longer surprise.

Critical inquiry in pursuit of explanation is a constructive outcome of surprise, transforming initial disorientation into motivated search. There is, as we have seen, no mechanical routine that guarantees success in the search for explanatory theory. Yet an emotional value of such search is to offer mature consolation for the stress of surprise and the renunciation of inadequate beliefs.[28] Achieving superordinate status in the economy of science, the value of inquiry becomes, indeed, autonomous, pressing new explanations deliberately into situations of risk, testing their vulnerability in novel ways, exposing their implicit predictions systematically to the chance of new surprise.

The constructive conquest of surprise is registered in the achievement of new explanatory structures, while cognitive application of these structures provokes surprise once more. Surprise is vanquished by theory, and theory is, in turn, overcome by surprise. Cognition is thus two-sided and has its own rhythm; it stabilizes and coordinates; it also unsettles and divides. It is responsible for shaping our patterned orientations to the future, but it must also be responsive to the insistent need to learn from the future. Establishing habits, it must stand ready to break them. Unlearning old ways of thought, it must also power the quest for new, and greater, expectations.[29] These stringent demands upon our cognitive processes also constitute stringent demands upon our emotional capacities. The growth of cognition is thus, in fact, inseparable from the education of the emotions.

Notes

1. For a discussion of this theme in the context of the history of American thought, see Morton White, *Science and Sentiment in America* (New York: Oxford University Press, 1972).

2. On this topic see R. S. Peters, "Reason and Passion," in *Education and the Development of Reason*, ed. R. F. Dearden, P. H. Hirst, and R. S. Peters (London: Routledge and Kegan Paul, 1972), especially the section on the rational passions, pp. 225–27. See also John Rawls, *A Theory of Justice* (Cambridge, Mass.: Harvard University Press, 1971), especially sections 67 and 73–75; P. Foot, "Moral Beliefs," *Proceedings of the Aristotelian Society* 59 (1958–59); and B.A.O. Williams, "Morality and the Emotions," in idem, *Problems of the Self* (Cambridge: Cambridge University Press, 1973). A significant recent book dealing

with a wide range of related topics is Robert C. Solomon, *The Passions* (New York: Doubleday, Anchor Press, 1976).

3. Cf. Aristotle, *Nicomachean Ethics,* book II, 3.

4. Peters, "Reason and Passion," p. 226.

5. John Dewey, *Human Nature and Conduct* (New York: Henry Holt, 1922, 1930), p. 196.

6. Ibid.

7. Related points are discussed in Peters, "Reason and Passion"; R. S. Peters, "The Education of the Emotions," in Dearden, Hirst, and Peters, *Education and the Development of Reason;* G. Pitcher, "Emotion," in Dearden, Hirst, and Peters, *Education and the Development of Reason;* and R. W. Hepburn, "The Arts and the Education of Feeling and Emotion," in Dearden, Hirst, and Peters, *Education and the Development of Reason.* See also W. P. Alston's article "Emotion and Feeling," in *The Encyclopedia of Philosophy* (New York: Macmillan, 1967), vol. 2, pp. 479–86.

8. Henry David Aiken, "Some Notes Concerning the Aesthetic and the Cognitive," *Journal of Aesthetics and Art Criticism* 13 (1955): 390–91.

9. Nelson Goodman, *Languages of Art* (Indianapolis, Ind.: Bobbs-Merrill [now Hackett], 1968), p. 248.

10. Ibid., p. 251.

11. Albert Einstein, "Autobiographical Notes," trans. P. A. Schilpp, in *Albert Einstein: Philosopher-Scientist,* ed. P. A. Schilpp (New York: Tudor Publishing, 1949), p. 7 (now published by the Open Court Publishing Company, LaSalle, Ill. The passage is quoted in a discussion of these and related points in I. Scheffler, *Science and Subjectivity* (Indianapolis, Ind.: Bobbs-Merrill [now Hackett], 1967), esp. chap. 4.

12. Carl G. Hempel, *Philosophy of Natural Science* (Englewood Cliffs, N.J.: Prentice-Hall, 1966), p. 16.

13. Michael Polanyi, *Personal Knowledge* (New York: Harper & Row, 1958, 1962), pp. 134–35.

14. Dewey, *Human Nature and Conduct,* p. 192.

15. For discussion helpful in clarifying certain points in this section, I am grateful to Professors Eli Hirsch and Jonas Soltis.

16. Moritz Schlick, "Über das Fundament der Erkenntnis," *Erenntnis* 4 (1934), trans. David Rynin, "The Foundations of Knowledge," in *Logical Positivism,* ed. A. J. Ayer (New York: Free Press, 1959).

17. Schlick, "Über das Fundament der Erkenntnis," in Ayer, ed., *Logical Positivism,* pp. 222–23. There is a general discussion of Schlick's paper in Scheffler, *Science and Subjectivity,* chap. 5.

18. Schlick, "Über das Fundament der Erkenntnis," in Ayer, ed., *Logical Positivism,* p. 227.

19. Scheffler, *Science and Subjectivity,* p. 30.

20. Jerome S. Bruner, J. J. Goodnow, and G. A. Austin, *A Study of Thinking* (New York: John Wiley, 1956), p. 47.

21. See N. R. Hanson, *Patterns of Discovery* (Cambridge: Cambridge University Press, 1958), pp. 18–19 and elsewhere. For a general discussion see Scheffler, *Science and Subjectivity,* esp. chaps. 1 and 2.

22. Ibid., chap. 2.

23. On these points, there is disagreement among previous writers. For informative historical as well as other material see M. M. Desai, "Surprise: A Historical and Experimental Study," *British Journal of Psychology Monograph Supplements*, no. 22 (1939); D. E. Berlyne, "Emotional Aspects of Learning," *Annual Review of Psychology* 15 (1964): 115–42; and W. R. Charlesworth, "The Role of Surprise in Cognitive Development," in *Studies in Cognitive Development*, ed. D. Elkind and J. H. Flavell (New York: Oxford University Press, 1969). Although I agree with various points in these psychological papers (e.g., Charlesworth, pp. 270 and 276), they tend to focus on individual behavior in a relatively local situation, whereas I tend to link surprise with failed prediction in the context of discussions in philosophy of science.

24. C. S. Peirce, "Some Consequences of Four Incapacities," in *Collected Papers of Charles Sanders Peirce,* ed. Charles Hartshorne and Paul Weiss, (Cambridge, Mass.: Harvard University Press, 1934), vol. 5, pp. 264–65. See also Israel Scheffler, *Four Pragmatists* (London: Routledge and Kegan Paul, 1974), pp. 52–53 and 69–70.

25. C. S. Peirce, "The Fixation of Belief," in Hartshorne and Weiss, eds., *Collected Papers of Charles Sanders Peirce,* 5: 382. See also a general discussion in Scheffler, *Four Pragmatists,* pp. 60ff.

26. Schlick, "Über das Fundament der Erkenntnis," in Ayer, ed., *Logical Positivism,* p. 223.

27. On explanation generally, see Israel Scheffler, *Anatomy of Inquiry* (New York: Alfred A. Knopf, 1963), pt. 1 (also Bobbs-Merrill [now Hackett], 1971). I use the term here in a very broad sense.

28. Interesting discussion of this sort of point and of related psychological issues is contained in Fay H. Sawyier, "About Surprise" (paper read to the annual meeting of the Western Division of the American Philosophical Association, St. Louis, Mo., 1974). For a discussion of the pedagogical use of surprise in the teaching of mathematics, see Stephen I. Brown, "Rationality, Irrationality and Surprise," *Mathematics Teaching: The Bulletin of the Association of Teachers of Mathematics,* no. 55 (Summer 1971).

29. On related points see the papers by H. Gardner, M. W. Wartofsky, and N. Goodman in *The Monist* 58 (1974): 319–42.

2

Human Nature and Potential

I. Education and the Language of Potential

The notion of potential is not only a hoary metaphysical idea that has come down to us from ancient Greek philosophy. It is also widely operative in the practical thinking of parents, educators, planners, and policy-makers in the contemporary world. Teachers, examiners, and counselors assess the potentials of students. Attributing the possession of given potentials to some, they deny it of others. But whereas lack of a given potential precludes its realization, possession of the same potential by no means guarantees it. Thus *attribution* of potential opens the further question of *realization:* what courses of study and training, what forms of practice or life experience would help given students to realize their evident potentials? This question is obviously of central importance to students, parents, educators, and planners.

Nor is this the only important question by any means. For not only may improvements be sought in the ways we try to *realize* a potential in fact possessed by a given student or group of students. We may also strive to help students *attain* potentials they have hitherto lacked. Possession as well as realization may, in other words, vary over time. A student now possessed of a given potential may or may not realize it in the future, but also a student now lacking such a potential may or may not come to possess it later on. The question of *enhancement* of a student's potentials thus goes beyond the question of their attribution or denial at a specific time. It follows that although the present lack of a given potential indeed precludes its realization now, it does not preclude its realization at a later time, when the potential in question may have been acquired.

This point is also, clearly, of critical importance to students, parents,

Delivered as the R. Freeman Butts Lecture at a meeting of The American Educational Studies Association in November 1982. It was published in *Educational Studies*, 14, no. 3 (1983): 211–24.

teachers, and planners: the stock of potentials changes over time. It is such change, so evident in contemporary education, that cuts most against the grain of the inherited notion of potential. Only if the fact of such change is ignored and the student's assessed potentials are taken as fixed and durable traits will his evident lacks be routinely mistaken for permanent educational deficiencies. The variation over time, whether of potentials or their realizations, has two important features requiring our immediate notice: the first is the contingency of such variation on human effort; the second is the influence of a given variation on later variations.

As to the contingency of variation on human effort, we have mentioned the important question, "What courses of study and training, what forms of practice or life experience would help given students to realize their evident potentials?" The normal presupposition of this question is that human activities of one or another sort may make a difference to realization. The design of appropriate studies, the provision of suitable training or experience, the will to learn and practice—all these and still other forms of effort may, in fact, vitally affect not only the realization but also the enhancement of potential. Thus, both what people potentially are and what they in fact turn out to be are contingent, to an incalculable extent, on human intention, both individual and social, bounded only by available resources and the limits of ingenuity. The burden of educational responsibility imposed on students, parents, teachers, planners, and, indeed, all society's members, stems from this fact.

The second significant feature of variation, noted above, is that any given variation influences subsequent ones. Potentials and their realizations are not isolated and discrete but intricately linked to one another. A girl who is potentially good at mathematics becomes a different person with actual achievement of mathematical skill. New potentials arise with the realization of the old; ways of thinking about related topics that formerly were closed are now open to her. New feelings of confidence may contribute to potentials for other sorts of learning as well.

The mere enhancement of potential in one area may moreover facilitate enhancement in another. A boy who has learned enough of a foreign language to be a potential translator of elementary texts has arrived at a new plateau; it is now easier for him than it was before to acquire the potential to translate more advanced texts or to compare the language in question analytically with his native tongue. The cunningly ordered sequence of potentials and realizations in any educational direction that may be chosen demands of the chooser foresight, breadth of vision, and a steady sense of value: foresight, because every educational change of state opens up new learning options it were well to anticipate; breadth of vision, because these options do not lie on a straight line determined by the initial subject, but radiate into different sectors of life; and a steady sense of value, because the choice of direction requires a grasp of complex alternative goods for comparison with one another, all more or less remote from the urgencies of the present. Foresight, vision, and value constitute the major part of wisdom; the task of the educator is thus revealed as rooted neither in convention, nor in craft, nor in caprice, but in a wisdom that unites knowledge, imagination, and the good.

The variation of potentials over time has been emphasized in the foregoing account as a way of bringing out questions of basic educational importance, and thus of outlining fundamental aspects of the educator's role. One such aspect, we have seen, has to do with the *enhancement*, or enlargement, of the stock of potentials of students. The student's assessed potentials as of now must not be taken in themselves to foreclose new acquisitions in the future. But another aspect related to variation has rather to do with the *shrinkage* of the present stock of potentials available to a person. Certain educational moments must be caught or they are gone forever. William James taught that character formation is a hardening of habits, that "by the age of thirty, the character has set like plaster, and will never soften again."[1] The moral he drew is that the nervous system, which functions thus, is to be made an ally of education rather than its enemy—education is to instill as many useful habits as early as possible, so that the hardening of character may then proceed in a desirable direction by its own momentum.

James's formulation of the point is no doubt overstated, but it strikingly expresses a general and genuine concern of modern educators. The capacity to learn is not an unlimited resource which can be lightly squandered. The child's curiosity, sufficiently blocked, may be dulled beyond awakening. The impulse to question, thwarted repeatedly, may eventually die. The flexibility of mind, adventurousness, and confidence required for exploring what is novel are precious and fragile learning instruments that lose their edge with disuse or abuse.

Moreover, aside from character and intellect, the existence of critical intervals for learning must be considered in widely diverse areas of education. Chess, the violin, and ballet must be learned early in life, not late; aspects of the visual system mature only within the bounds of relevant critical periods; beyond another such period, any learning of a new language will, in all probability, carry with it the acquisition of a spoken accent. Potentials here today may, in short, be gone tomorrow.

The educator must thus not only anticipate and promote the emergence of potentials not yet in evidence, but also try to capitalize to the fullest on potentials now manifest but shortly to disappear. He must combine a hopeful imagination of students' future potentials with a realistic appreciation of those potentials that are now, perhaps only temporarily, possessed. Striving to overcome present lacks through future possibilities, the educator is also constantly haunted by the specter of past opportunity wasted. The pressure of educational time forces him to look in both directions at once.

The mention of wasted opportunity will be instantly recognized by every reflective parent and teacher as marking a basic preoccupation. Time is so short, resources so few, education so precious in shaping the child's life: has everything possible been done to nurture the fragile growth? The child's own view is foreshortened, its sense of time and change truncated, its things taken for granted as fixed. The illusion of the rightness and durability of the given and the overestimation of the child's own powers have yet to be tempered by further experience. The child cannot be expected to be sensitive to the question of wasted opportunity. But to concerned parents and teachers viewing the child against the backdrop of a longer and more realistic time line, the question can never be far below the surface. And it is a question often formulated in terms of the concept of potential. Have we passed the critical period for any of the child's potentials that are important? Have we failed to spot or appreciate crucial potentials through our own blindness? Have valuable potentials remained hidden through lack of general knowledge or lack of social interest? Have apathy, or poverty, or bias, or misguided policy thwarted the appraisal of children's potentials and cruelly closed off their life prospects? Such worries, natural to parents and teachers, are central also to the concerns of society at large, for whatever opens and closes the life prospects of children determines the direction and quality of society itself. Thus the process of educational planning, through which a society mediates its treatment of children's potentials, is in its style and scope an index of the society's self-image.

The press of educational responsibility is indeed heavy and relentless. Demanding relief, the educational decision-maker would welcome any way to lighten the load, to lessen the onus of choice. The tendency to replace wisdom with technology thus becomes understandable, promising to reduce the subtleties of complex decision to the simplicities of formula. We have noted the simplifying myth of fixed potentials which, inherited along with the ancient vocabulary of potential, still thrives in various quarters, although defeated by the facts of change.

A more general strategy of relief, also encouraged by traditional precedent, is to hide the necessity of discriminating among the potentials of a student—to assume them all to be harmoniously realizable. Thus the educator does not need to evaluate alternative combinations of potentials for attempted realization. His job is simply to identify the potentials that are there and then to promote the realization of all in the most efficient manner. Maximal self-realization is the goal, understood as the fulfillment of all of one's potentials, satisfying every one of one's potentialities—"*being*," as the saying goes, "all that one *can* be."

The problem of education, thus understood, is largely emptied of its evaluative aspects and reduced to a question of fact coupled with a question of technology. The question of fact is: What potentials does the student have? The question of technology is: How are these potentials most efficiently to be realized? Both questions can, in principle, be turned over to scientific investigation for resolution and the educator's task reduced to doing whatever the investigation concludes will most efficiently realize all the student's potentials, there being some such self-realizing course available in every case. Thus are the main functions of education reduced to *finding* the potentials and then *realizing* them forthwith.

Comforting as this picture has been for both educational theorists and practitioners, it is fatally flawed. William James expressed the main point when he somewhere remarked that "the philosopher and the lady-killer cannot both keep house in the same tenement of clay." The potential for the one career and the potential for the other may both be genuinely *possessed* by a given youth but they are not, alas, jointly *realizable*. Merely to *identify* these potentials is thus not sufficient to warrant the attempt at realization. For to realize the one has the effect of precluding the other, the two being unrealizable together. If one is to be preferred to the other, there must be a judgment embodying such preference. And such judgment, if sufficiently reflective, will involve considerations of relative value affecting the conflicting realizations in question—some reference to imagined alternative goods between which choice must decide.

Every student in fact harbors potentials that are, as such, compatible, but whose realizations conflict. One cannot literally be all that one can be; there are fundamentally different lives that anyone might live, depending on the choices made by oneself and others—and it is true of many such lives that each excludes the rest. Choice precludes as well as includes; there is no blinking this fact and, consequently, no relief from educational responsibility in the notion of a comprehensive fulfillment of all one's potentials.

Nor does this notion represent the only way in which the concept of potential is employed so as to lessen the pressure of choice. The educational preoccupations we have outlined above concern the proper attribution and enhancement of potential, the reduction of shrinkage of potential, the discovery and development of hidden potentials, and the efficient realization of potentials. In every one of these cases, the potentials in question are assumed to have positive value and their realizations to represent goods as well. Yet the assumption, once questioned, is seen to be groundless. People are potentially evil as well as good. They are potentially considerate but also potentially callous, potentially kind and potentially cruel, potentially sensitive and potentially boorish, potentially insightful and intelligent, and potentially obtuse and stupid.

In the typical practical employment of the language of potential, these negative aspects are all filtered out. It is not noted that the educator's aim is to destroy as well as to strengthen potentials, to shrink as well as to enhance various sorts, to block as well as to promote their realization. Propped by the classical philosophical tradition in which the concept of potential was originally nurtured, this reading of the concept accentuates the positive, fostering the illusion that no value discriminations by the educator are needed. All that wants doing is the factual identification of existent potentials, all to be promoted for all are worthy—all aspects of the real, or higher, self to be realized in education.[2]

II. Potential and Human Nature

To criticize such uses of the traditional language of potential, however, neither answers the needs that this language has met in practice nor acknowledges the basis in human nature from which these needs have sprung. What features of human nature indeed underlie the appeal of the notion of potential in educational thinking?

Behind all such use of the notion lies the basic reality that human beings are not constrained in their development as are other animals. Their lives are not bounded by the reach of their instincts and drives, coupled with the opportunities of their physical environments. They do not live in the immediate present alone, responding only to the current forces playing upon them. Human beings are symbolic animals, creators and creatures of culture, capable of memory, imagination, fear, and hope, interpreters of the world and of themselves, choosers among options they themselves define, and vulnerable as well to the choices of their fellows. Such interpretations and choices make a fateful difference in the direction and quality of a human life. What the biology of the infant leaves open at birth is, in short, filled out by culture, history, education, and decision.

The realization of this fact leads us to think of the particular dependent infant as having an array of possible futures, the selection among which depends in good part upon what we do. Some such futures we may deem intrinsic to the child's nature and thus value them as his possible achievements, others we deem foreign to his nature or otherwise unfortunate. We tend then to categorize the former as his potentials and to train all our efforts on their optimal realization. Conversely, an abstractly valuable future that we judge to be beyond a given infant's reach is one we need expend no effort on, and we can ignore it with an easy conscience, if not without regret.

Although such ways of thinking are understandable, they are nevertheless in urgent need of critical examination and analysis. They are historical residues of the Aristotelian metaphysic of essences defining natural kinds. The properties intrinsic to the natural kind constitute its essence, at once defining its natural goal and norm, and explaining its development; thus thought Aristotle. The problems with this doctrine are, first of all, that the notions of essence, natural kind, and natural goal are unclear and untestable, yielding no consequence amenable to experimental or observational control; second, that natural kinds and essences are fixed, offering no way to accommodate the facts of change; and third, that the presupposed connections of essence with value are dubious: (a) that it is of the "essence" of an egg to become a chicken does not mean it ought not become an omelette; and (b) that a person has evil traits can be reconciled with his essence only by implausibly construing all such traits as lacks or privations.

The notion of potential in educational parlance is subject to analogous troubles: what is the criterion for judging that a given feature is *intrinsic* to a child's nature? Assuming that we judge some feature to be intrinsic, how does it explain how the child actually develops? How does the idea of an intrinsic nature account for the flexibility and change characteristic of actual personal development? And why does the intrinsic character of a feature show that it is valuable? In practice, as we have seen, the value of "potentialities" is in fact presupposed as an additional premise. The notion that if we only had a scientific method for finding the *facts* about potential, we would then have a guide for *value judgment* is thus a notion that has to be given up.

III. Three Reconstructions of Potential

My purpose is not to defend traditional or current uses of the notion of potential. If the above criticisms are correct, we have indeed to be especially aware of its pitfalls. Used in educational theory and social planning, the notions of intrinsic natures, fixed potentials, or essential talents offer untestable devices for projecting a limited and rigid view of human possibilities. They hold out the will-o'-the-wisp of a neutral science by which our values can be determined without our need to take moral responsibility; and they offer meanwhile a convenient screen by which we can mask our value choices not only from others but even from ourselves.

We must nevertheless recognize the human situations that give point to the notion of potential. Acknowledging its motivation and functions in educational decision-making, we can strive so to reconstruct it as to free it of the older difficulties and thus improve its functioning in such context. Reconstruction is, in effect, replacement: new conceptualizations to substitute for the old. I want, in this spirit, to suggest three reconstructed notions of potential, a *capacity* notion, a *predictive* notion, and a *decision* notion. My hope is that these notions, taken jointly, may prove adequate to fulfill the positive functions of the traditional conception, while avoiding its fundamental difficulties. The reconstructions to follow are thus to be treated as philosophical hypotheses aimed at improving our inherited apparatus for educational description and, ultimately, educational decision. I hope, in particular, that the notions to be proposed may be applied in a testable manner, free of covert value implications, that they may be compatible with the facts of developmental change, and that they may prove useful in guiding educational inquiry and clarifying educational choice.

Let me begin by observing that the notion of *potential* ordinarily refers, not to existing or manifest capacities, skills, or other traits that a person may have, but rather to the possible future learning, development, or acquisition of such features. To say of John that he is now a *pianist* (or explicitly that he can now play the piano) ascribes to him now the capacity or ability to play. On the other hand, to say of John that he is now a *potential* pianist does not imply that he now has the ability to play. Indeed, it implies that he cannot now play, but it says more than just that he now lacks the ability. What else then can be implied? Presumably that he has the "makings" of a pianist in the future. But what exactly does this mean?

It seems to be a sensible assertion, surely. For, of all those people who cannot now play the piano, some differ from the rest in being potential pianists. But how is this difference to be interpreted? To suppose that there is some essence of piano playing that they alone possess, some occult seed of piano talent now germinating inside them or a ghostly pianist already performing inside their souls, is sheer nonsense.

Perhaps, then, we are predicting of the potential pianists that they will acquire the ability to play at some time in the future, while those others who are not potential pianists will not. This is, at any rate, a clear distinction, but it is not the one we seek. For John may be a potential pianist and never in fact become a pianist at any time in the future. It is perfectly consistent to speak of unrealized potentials; it follows that to ascribe a potential is not in itself to make a categorical prediction that the potential will be realized.

In short, if a potentiality-attribution is indeed a sensible assertion but neither ascribes an essence nor makes a categorical prediction, how exactly is its content to be construed? This is the basic conceptual problem to be faced. Unless we resolve this problem, we cannot hope to be clear about the issues at stake in any particular dispute over potential. Nor can we be clear about the evidence required to evaluate potential or the assumptions presupposed in claims to potential. Without a clarification of the meaning of our concept, the logic of its use must remain opaque.

Let us then have another look at the notion of capacity. To say that John is a potential pianist denies that he has the capacity to play the piano, but says something more in addition. The problem is: What else? My first proposal is that it says that John has the *capacity to become* a pianist. He has now no capacity to play but he has the capacity to acquire the capacity to play, i.e., to learn how to play, to develop into a player. We thus contrast the *manifest capacity* with the *capacity to achieve it*.

Moreover, this proposal can be generalized. For we can apply it not only to the acquisition of capacities (such as playing the piano) but also to the acquisition of habits, traits, propensities, and other characteristics. Thus, a person may be described as having the potential for understanding differential equations or as being a potentially heavy smoker, or as a potentially well-informed citizen, etc. In general, then, the proposal interprets the *potential* possession of a characteristic at a given time as implying its *manifest lack* at that time and asserting in addition the capacity to acquire the characteristic in question at some time in the future. Potentiality is, in short, taken as a subtype of *capacity,* that is, the *capacity to acquire* a specified characteristic.

How is *capacity* itself to be interpreted? I understand capacity as the denial of a constraint. Capacity is a sort of possibility; to say it is *possible* that such-and-such is to say that it is not *necessary* that *not* such-and-such. Similarly, to assert the capacity for a certain outcome is frequently just to deny that the outcome in question will necessarily not occur.[3]

Skilled performances, for example, require the coordination of several factors beyond the mere decision to perform; they require, for example, a permissive environment, appropriate means, minimal know-how. If any required factor is missing, the performance will be *prevented;* if we know such a factor is absent, we have good reason to suppose that the performance will not take place—because it *cannot.* Any one of a number of different preventive circumstances may block a given performance. I may say I can't drive today, knowing my car is in the repair shop; on another occasion I may say I can't drive, because my arm is in a cast. Now, to negate the assertion that John *can't* drive is to say he *can,* that is, he has the *capacity* to drive. And this is in turn to deny that some relevant preventive circumstance obtains, relevance being determined by the particular context. But clearly, to assert that John *can* drive does not predict that he *will;* it just denies the necessity that he *won't.*

Now, the acquisition of a skill or a trait is also preventable by a variety of circumstances. Such acquisition also depends on the coordination of several factors, the absence of any of which will provide good reason to suppose the acquisition will be blocked. No less than *driving* itself, *learning to drive* may be prevented by any of a variety of circumstances. To *deny* that a given preventive circumstance, relevant in context, obtains is thus to *affirm* the capacity for learning to drive, the capacity to acquire driving skill—to become a driver. And this, according to my first proposal, is what it means to say that someone is a *potential* driver.

To study potential, under this proposal, is thus to study the *capacity for acquisition* of features of various sorts. This, in turn, is to study which factors may *impede* acquisition, learning, or development of such features, which conditions constitute preventive circumstances. To investigate potential is thus, for example, to investigate such biologically preventive factors impeding learning as nutritional deficiencies, sensory or motor deprivation, damage to the nervous system, birth defects, etc. It is also to inquire into cultural factors that are preventive, in particular, belief systems, institutions, and policies that may impede acquisition. An important general point of interest is that *false* beliefs about preventive circumstances for a given trait may themselves become preventive for that trait. For example, a false belief that women cannot, for reasons of physiology, acquire mechanical skills may itself become a circumstance blocking such acquisition, especially when enshrined in policy and in social and educational institutions. Another general point of critical importance is that the potentialities truly attributed to a person or group are relative to the social circumstances assumed to be in place.

I turn now to a *predictive* reconstruction of potential. When we say someone has a *tendency or propensity,* rather than just a *capacity,* to swim, we do not simply deny the existence of some preventive circumstance. But we make no categorical prediction of swimming either. What we often do is to make a *conditional* prediction: *if* he has the chance *and* is not prevented, he is likely to swim.

Some potentiality-attributions seem to have a similar character. To say that Jones is a potential heart-attack victim does not say just that nothing prevents him from having a heart attack. Nor does it make the categorical prediction that Jones *will* in fact be a heart-attack victim. What additional content can the statement then have, short of categorical prediction? Here the notion of conditional prediction suggests itself. If certain (more or less vaguely specified) conditions continue to hold true of him, the available evidence makes a heart attack likely. He is "at risk" relative to certain conditions, *to a degree* in principle testable by statistical evidence.

The general idea behind my second proposal is then to take *propensity for acquisition* of various features as the basis for certain potentiality assertions, as I earlier took *capacity for acquisition* as the basis for certain others. A statement asserting such a propensity will in turn be understandable not as affirming a capacity but as making a conditional prediction of the acquisition in question.

Conditional predictions may themselves be chained to form sequential predictions. Such chains leading to a given acquisition provide a means of interpreting the psychologically important concept of *development*. For a given acquisition target state, we may be in no position to say of John that if certain initial state conditions hold of him at a certain time he can be predicted to reach the target state at a certain later time. We may, however, be able to provide such a conditional prediction carrying him to an intermediate state, and then, given such state plus the assumption of further conditions at that time, to predict the target itself conditionally. In similar fashion, any number of intermediate states may theoretically be chained together to form a developmental sequence. Thus, from x's initial state s_1 we predict intermediate state s_2; from x's state s_2, plus simultaneous conditions c_2, we predict s_3, etc., and from $s_n - 1$, plus simultaneous conditions $c_n - 1$, we predict the target state s_n.[4]

To study potential, under this proposal, is to study such sequences: What laws are empirically available for predicting the states s in question, what specifications of persons x and of conditions c are presupposed? Where empirical information is currently lacking to support a developmental picture of acquisition, what sorts of information are needed to fill out the schema? As before, we note the importance of studying conditions of a biological as well as a cultural sort. And, as before, we emphasize that the beliefs and expectations of x and of others relating to x may themselves constitute significant factors in developmental sequences. This fact is relevant not only to the importance of the agent's own attitude in learning, but also to the significance of the attitudes of others, e.g., the "Pygmalion effect." It is relevant also to the question of policy formation, that is, the deliberate intervention to produce or withhold an intermediate condition subject to social manipulation.

Let us attend, finally, to a third reconstruction of potential—in terms of decision. We focus, in particular, on those conditional predictions in which the agent's own decision constitutes a critical factor in acquisition. Consider a skilled performer in an environment that is permissive, i.e., that does not prevent the performance in question. Beyond the *capacity* to perform, relative to such an environment, the skilled performer also has *capability*. That is, he can be generally *relied on* to perform properly under these circumstances, *if* he chooses. A less skilled performer is distinguishable by a lower degree of reliability in producing proper performances at will. Thus, two archers of unequal skill show differing reliability in hitting the target under the same environmental conditions, when they are both in fact *trying* to hit the target.

The factor of *skill,* or, more generally, *capability,* brings the performance within the power or control of the agent—within the range of his or her decision. To the degree that a person is capable, then—assuming no positive prevention—if he decides to produce the outcome in question, he is likely to do so. Capability thus allows a special kind of conditional prediction, one in which the person's own decision enables us to predict the outcome with a fair degree of confidence.

I hold this sort of conditional prediction to be of special interest. For it places the agent's own decision at the center of consideration, rather than supposing him to be simply a passive recipient of external influences playing upon him. Enhancement of the agent's capability increases his choice of options and so, in one clear sense, his freedom. Lacking the capability of hitting the target, his decision is ineffective; he cannot effectively choose to hit it, even under permissive circumstances. With the capability, this choice opens up for the first time, and with it a new access of freedom.

Now my third proposal is to interpret potential as the *capability of acquiring* new learnings. To speak, in this vein, of a student's *potential* to be an athlete, a mathematician, or a carpenter, is to refer to the student's capability to learn what is needed. Given that biology and culture do not impede, the question of potential is the question whether the student can be expected to learn what he or she decides to learn. To increase potential in this sense is to put the means of learning within the person's own decision range, to provide the basic skills, the prerequisite knowledge and attitudes for learning. It is to empower the agent to learn, making the agent's self-determination more effective through putting varied skills and traits within range of his own choice.

The study of potential, under this proposal, is the study of conditions that empower learning. Beyond the creation of externally permissive environments, what factors strengthen or weaken the agent's capability to learn? What are the basic arts and skills ingredient in learning of various sorts and how may they be fostered? We are here, in sum, concerned with the effective use a person may make of the social opportunities he is provided—with his *capability* to take advantage of environmental *capacity*.

This concludes the sketch of my three reconstructed notions of potential. I do not claim that any one or any combination of these notions is synonymous with the traditional conception. But I do claim that, together, they may serve to advance the clarification of educational possibility, compatibly with the facts of human change and the responsibilities of value decision. Whether my claim indeed realizes such potential of its own is, however, for future discussion to determine.[5]

Notes

1. William James, *The Principles of Psychology* (1890; reprint, New York: Dover, 1950), vol. 1, pp. 121–22. On James's view of habit, see my *Four Pragmatists* (London: Routledge and Kegan Paul, 1974) pp. 122ff.

2. On these and related points, see John Passmore, *The Perfectibility of Man* (London: Duckworth, 1970), pp. 18–19 and elsewhere.

3. For a general discussion, see Gilbert Ryle, *The Concept of Mind* (London: Hutchinson, 1949), pp. 126ff. My treatment of capacity and preventive circumstances here draws on chapter 5 of my *Conditions of Knowledge* (Chicago: University of Chicago Press, 1965), pp. 91ff.

4. The idea is set forth as an account of genetic explanation in history in C. G. Hempel, *Aspects of Scientific Explanation* (New York: Free Press, 1965), pp. 447–53, and in Ernest Nagel, *The Structure of Science* (New York: Harcourt, 1961), pp. 564–68.

5. This paper presented a first published outline of ideas later elaborated in my book *Of Human Potential* (London: Routledge, 1985). I there refer to the predictive notion of potential as a *propensity* notion, and I refer to the decision notion as a *capability* notion.

3

Making and Understanding

I. See How it Was Made

If I made it, I must understand it. This idea, or something like it, seems to underlie, consciously or unconsciously, a good deal of educational practice. Get underneath or behind the product, see how it was made, and you will appreciate it, we tell the student, emphasizing the originating process, method, or procedure. See how the proof was arrived at, the performance conducted, the statue sculpted, the painting painted, the theory constructed and chosen. A product remains opaque until seen as embodiment of plan and skill, analyzed as artifact.

To call it a product is, indeed, already to view it as artifact, though not yet to understand it as such. The relevant understanding arises from reconstructing the steps by which the work was created, dismembering the product in imagination into its elements and scattering them backward in time, then reliving the steps one by one in which each element was put in place. Thus reenacting the creator's teleological process, you grasp the intelligence that went into each step of construction, seeing how each figured in the maker's mind as serving some purpose in accord with a principle of strategy or choice.

In understanding a mathematical proof, this means seeing its motivation line by line, "the end from afar"—as Poincaré put it—and not merely the *post facto* justification of the line by logic. Grasping the motivation of a proof yields understanding in that it locates each line within a general framework of strategic principles. Without such understanding, one would, in Poincaré's words, be "like a writer well up in grammar but destitute of ideas."[1] With such understanding, one can see similar lines in other proofs

Reprinted from *Proceedings of the Philosophy of Education Society*, 1987. I am grateful to Catherine Z. Elgin, Kenneth S. Hawes, and Vernon A. Howard for helpful comments on an earlier version.

in the same developmental light. These proofs are no longer inert logical objects; they have become outcomes of intelligent choice.

In understanding a product of physical rather than mathematical construction, it is again the strategic element that gives understanding, over and above mere causality. To see how the carpenter's prefigured end is realized in the cabinet through his intelligent use of causal factors is what gives understanding or appreciation of the product: we see it not merely as caused, but as caused by intelligent action in pursuit of a purpose. Grasping the strategy of such action, we can view its outcome as an embodiment of intelligence.

Reenactive understanding of the creator's process yields a new perception of the product. Children under a certain age, so I am told, do not realize that paintings are not "natural" objects—things found as such in nature. The eventual realization that they are *made* opens up a whole new perspective. Learning how musical instruments work brings a new sensitivity to the act of listening to music, aiding one to perceive it as a product of skill. Listening is now not inert but active; appreciation is no longer mesmerized by surface qualities, but grasps these qualities as outcomes of judgment, as created by intelligence.

Analogous points can be made about still other realms. Reading with understanding, for example, requires getting behind the cold print of a newspaper or textbook—seeing it as an item of manufacture: somebody chose to put such and such words together to make the whole. What vision, what purposes, and what decisions governed this process? Critical approaches to recorded history, journalism, literature, and the social sciences depend on the activation of this question by readers.

The understanding of a historical action as distinct from written history is, similarly, a matter of reconstructing its rationale, the framework of reasons and principles that motivated its occurrence. The notion of reenactment, indeed, figures centrally in the thought of Collingwood, who describes the historian trying to understand Caesar's actions as "envisaging for himself the situation in which Caesar stood, and thinking for himself what Caesar thought about the situation and the possible ways of dealing with it. The history of thought, and therefore all history," concludes Collingwood, "is the re-enactment of past thought in the historian's own mind."[2]

Finally, to appreciate the corpus of scientific knowledge is to see how its making was guided by strategy, in accord with method, and in line with presumed purpose. "Learning to think as a scientist does"—the slogan of the inquiry movement in curriculum—had the aim of enhancing understanding through the sort of reenactive rehearsal I have sketched.

Projected onto the cosmic realm, the idea takes on familiar theological outline. God understands His creatures perfectly because He was, as Maimonides put it, "guided by his knowledge in the act of" creating them.[3] We, merely creatures, cannot reenact God's process of creation or fathom His purposes. Our knowledge, dependent on limited observation of His products, is therefore radically imperfect. Within our own limited sphere, however, we create things and deeds as well, fitting means to ends, processes to outcomes in appropriate ways, thus displaying understanding at a level commensurate with human capabilities. In this limited creativity, we display our Divine origins, the intelligence which is the image of God implanted within us. Nor does the theistic idiom belong only to an archaic age of belief. Scientists as well as philosophers have been often captivated by the idea of a tight web of necessity binding all things together, of which we may achieve only partial glimpses through science. From Newton to Einstein, the teleological idiom has seemed apt in expressing this situation. Thus Einstein's God "does not play dice with the world," nor is He "malicious," although He is surely "subtle." Our own understanding, striving to fathom the structure of the universe, is thus conceived as trying to grasp the principles of its rational construction.[4]

II. Process is not Enough

There are cracks in the picture so far painted. To understand the product, we have said, we must see how it was made, come to know the rationale by which each step in its creation was guided; otherwise the product is opaque. But creation seems not, in general, to be exhaustively divisible into motivated steps. A product is more than the sum of such steps, incorporating, as it does, influences beyond the maker's control. Even a rigorous mathematical proof, conceived as product, outstrips its initiating strategy, there being no decision procedure for the construction of proofs, and supplementary heuristics being sketchy and incomplete. "In school arithmetic," writes Quine, "everything we want to know can be determined by mechanical computation. In advanced mathematics, on the other hand, proofs have in large part to be discovered by artistry and good fortune," and "we may despite all efforts fail to assure ourselves of some validity or implication which actually holds, simply for lack of luck or ingenuity in hitting upon the appropriate deduction."[5]

Now if, by sheer luck, the appropriate deduction *has* been "hit upon," it will hardly be possible to refer it to some motivating strategy beyond the vacuous principle "Try, try again!" If indeed, then, understanding the proof requires reference throughout to nonvacuous strategic principles, the proof is beyond understanding. Alternatively, we must concede that understanding the proof is not, after all, dependent upon grasping, for each step, the rationale of its construction. Such construction is not merely a teleological chain of decisions according to principle; something in the nature of guesswork and "good fortune" must be acknowledged as well.

God is, of course, not in this predicament since He necessarily sees the truth of the theorem from eternity. But if He consequently needs no guesswork, the very eternity of His seeing removes His need for proof altogether. And even God cannot produce a decision procedure for human beings, to replace their reliance on proof. According to Kronecker, God made the natural numbers, man made all the rest. But the human dependence on proof in mathematics can be overcome neither by Divine nor by human decree.

When we turn from mathematics to science, the limitations of strategy are even more evident. Theory is no stepwise result of a sequential choice process. "Thinking as a physicist does" means engaging in what Einstein called "a free play with concepts,"[6] such play itself irreducible to exhaustive series of rational choices according to nonvacuous strategic principles. The product of the physicist's creation thus cannot be understood wholly as an outcome of such choices. If we are to resist the conclusion that it therefore cannot be understood at all, we must allow that understanding physics goes beyond a grasp of the process by which it was created, at least as process has so far been interpreted.

A misleading suggestion of the inquiry movement, no doubt unintended, is that once the pupil has learned to think as a physicist does, he or she should be able to generate current physical theory, given only a sufficient supply of data. But because Einstein's free play with concepts was an essential element of his achievement, all the training in the world in inquiry methods would not provide a basis for expecting the pupil to repeat that achievement. One could nevertheless properly expect the pupil to acquire an *understanding* of Einstein's theory without having to reenact its construction. Physics is, in effect, one might say, not solely a "logical" product but a "historical" one as well; its current shape derives, in part, from the free play activities of innumerable historical physicists.

Nor does anyone suppose that the arts that we have have arisen through the application of strategic principles to given data. Learning to think as an artist does will not lead you to paint *Guernica* or *Le Déjeuner sur l'Herbe*. The history of art is required to explain the distinctive features of our artistic heritage. Beyond the skill and discipline of historical artists, the content of their imaginations must, in any case, be registered for any adequate account to emerge.

See how far we have now come. We began with the idea that understanding rests on teleological reenactment, and we are now saying that such understanding rests at least in part on historical brute fact—on seeing what free play has wrought in the minds of historical agents. We are thus appealing to causality rather than teleology, surrendering the original idea that a product is opaque until seen as wholly an embodiment of plan and skill—as intention intelligently realized.

III. A Salvage Attempt and its Breakdown

A concession may be offered, in order to salvage at least part of the original idea: it will be granted that *discipline* is indeed only one aspect of science and art, to be supplemented by *freedom* in creation. Once freedom has been exercised, however, then discipline alone comes into play. Thus arises a familiar division between pure and applied science, and an analogous separation of inspiration and execution in art. In science, free play is conceded a place in the generation of theory, but not in its application. Once a theory is available, applying it becomes merely a matter of disciplined intelligence or skill, and teleological rationality rules. The engineer, the architect, the physician, the carpenter, the professional or artisan in every field is to be sharply distinguished from the originator of the fundamental theory upon which his or her practice rests. In applying such fundamental theory, the practitioner indeed creates, but the resultant product of application can be wholly understood as an outcome of skill.

Similarly—in the spirit of Collingwood's separation of art from craft[7]—the artist is conceded freedom in conceiving his basic idea, but once the idea is available, the rest is merely a matter of disciplined execution, a display of technical prowess at best. Thus, once we separate the *making of fundamental ideas* from the *making of things in accordance with such ideas,* we can save teleological reenactment as the basis of understanding, at least with reference to the latter sort of making. Familiar conceptions of professional training are indeed founded on such a separation, and the theological metaphor resonates behind it: God's will is free, but the realization of whatever He wills is necessary. We may not fathom his purpose but we can, partially at least, sense its orderly execution.

This critical division between freedom and discipline will not, however, support the desired thesis. Even if we grant that theory generation is distinguishable from theory application, it does not follow that such application is analyzable into teleologically rational steps. God's creation, a necessary outcome of His will, can carry no surprises for Him. But human creation is always contingent, always experimental, always capable of yielding surprises—not only for others, but for the human creator himself. The product humanly made is never a pure function of creative purpose and foreseeable consequences of the maker's actions. The human maker does not fully own his own product. Understanding it is therefore not reducible to grasping the steps that went into its making.

The experimental character of application may be seen in the fact that presupposed theories are not guaranteed to work as intended. Where such intention is thwarted, the product may deviate from the maker's initial vision. Neither the finished house nor the finished aria is wholly a function of its maker's intention. He will indeed have made the product but he will not have seen how it would emerge from his hands. To view his creation solely through the lens of his initial intention thus gives a false representation of it. Rectifying such representation requires taking into account additional circumstances over and above his intention.

God, unlike mortals, needs no education; He does not and cannot learn from experience, as He necessarily knows all from eternity. Human beings are, however, never in a position to assume that no breakdowns of their theories will occur in application, hence never in a position to discount further experience. On the contrary, breakdowns are to be anticipated when theories are applied, and such breakdowns, located and scrutinized, constitute an invaluable educational resource.

IV. Dreamers, Robots, and Surprise

The general point holds not only for scientific applications but also for artistic creation, for policy-making, and for everyday activity as well. The artist is not a composite of dreamer and robot, the dreamer intuiting the idea and the robot executing it automatically in the chosen medium. The painter or composer does not first thrill to a new conception and then thoughtlessly stamp it on his raw material; rather, he tries it out on the material, which reshapes him as he reshapes it. His thinking is not limited to the first phase of his making; it permeates every stage, the results of his every move requiring fresh evaluation and a reconsidering of basic directions.

Such interaction of idea and result is no less important in policy-making than it is in the sciences and the arts. Policy conceived may be expected to go awry in application. Alert intelligence is thus required at the very point of translation into action. Instead, having invested energy and pride in the drafting of policies, institutions often proceed to shelter them from experimental scrutiny. Similarly, in carrying out our day-to-day activities, we find it difficult to treat our underlying presumptions experimentally, shielding ourselves from the very surprises that may further educate us.

The aversion to surprise indeed runs deep. Surely, according to the popular myth, our technology can be made foolproof and surprises avoided: breakdowns of theory can, after all, themselves be predicted, and thus averted or otherwise accommodated by our plans. It is thus that defects in an automobile design are foretold before the car is put into production and avoided by using a different design. Alternatively, the defect, once realized, may be coped with by compensating devices. In either case, we need fear no surprises in the application of ideas.

The trouble is that we are always one step behind. Past breakdowns can indeed be analyzed, and their likelihoods can then be built into the underlying theory of the product. But there is no guarantee that *past* breakdowns are the *only* sorts that will occur. Like every theory, the theory of past breakdowns may itself be faulty or incomplete. Further, the very concept of a *breakdown* is not one that can be readily circumscribed in advance, being itself a teleological notion and varying as people's purposes, values, or expectations vary. A defect in car design must be thought of not purely in engineering terms but in human terms, for what counts as a defect depends on what expectations users may have.

The upshot is that surprises in application cannot be precluded; there is no point at which we can simply apply, make, or act, with full immunity to unforeseeable consequences. Cars may be pretested, projects put through pilot-study stages, appliances experimentally run until they fail so the causes can be analyzed—but further surprise cannot be ruled out. Every application of an idea is a pretest, every project a pilot project, every new failure an occasion for further retrospective analysis.[8]

V. Products Understood Independently

The idea that insight into process underlies understanding of the product thus seems to suffer from two major defects. First, the element of free play needs to be registered in addition to process. Second, even taking free play into account, the product is not wholly a function of the maker's purpose and the foreseeable consequences of his activity. It harbors objective surprises that go beyond the maker's perspective. These defects show that insight into process, i.e., into the foreseeable consequences of the maker's actions, is not *sufficient* for an understanding of the product. But, moreover, neither is such insight *necessary*. For the product can be understood independently.

Such independent understanding is not hard to conceive. The product has, after all, its own life and its own features; it is an *object*, not an *aspect*. As such, it is perceivable not just from the maker's angle of vision, but from multiple other vantage points. It can be walked around, looked at from many sides as well as from below and above, triangulated, tested for its functions and effects, thrown into new combinations with other objects and novel purposes, and assessed for its prospective uses and associations as well as its retrospective background.

The understanding of Einstein's or any other theory is a matter of seeing how it works, what it entails, what it denies, what it enables, what can be said for it, and what against it. Understanding a text is a matter of gauging what it means and not what the author meant, for an author may intend something not in fact said and say something not in fact meant. Once the text is produced, it is objectified, released, given birth, assuming its own career beyond the maker's control. To understand it is to see its structure, its organization, its references, its various interpretations and not, in particular, its historical and developmental origins.

Why, then, does education lay such stress on process? Is this emphasis wholly misguided, a product of illusion merely? I think the answer is no, and I shall try, in the following sections, to say why.

VI. Process Reconceived

First of all, the initial construal of process, both by defenders and critics in the foregoing discussion, has been unduly narrow. This construal has in turn forced an overly narrow construction on the notions of reenactment and strategy. Process has, in effect, been portrayed as a *generative* procedure, a function generating a subsequent state out of a given state—a line in a proof out of previous lines, a theory out of data, an action given relevant circumstances, a physical operation when initial conditions are specified. This portrayal excludes free play in science, artistry and good fortune in proof, and creative invention in art as altogether beyond process and alien to strategic considerations. It further encourages us to interpret reenactment as duplication from scratch, a *creatio ex nihilo* of the achievements of the past.

But if, as in our previous example, the right mathematical deduction has been hit upon by sheer luck, rather than by use of a generative procedure, that is not the end of the story so far as a grasp of the process goes. A lucky strike has to be *recognized* as such; the happy deduction needs to be *seen* as right—not simply as valid by reference to earlier lines but as motivated, i.e., as marking an advance toward the desired goal. The purpose of reaching that goal does not generate the lucky strike, but it defines the direction that such a strike must follow; strategic considerations, further, explain why a given move, no matter how generated, constitutes an advance toward the goal. Such considerations do not look back to origins, but serve rather to monitor and evaluate the course of thought by reference to its bearing on the envisaged future. More broadly understood, then, process may be taken to include not just generative procedures, but also evaluative strategies; it is thus altogether compatible with free play, good fortune, and sheer luck. In consequence, the reenactment it invites is not a *duplication* of the lucky strike, whether in science, mathematics, or art, but rather a grasp of its mode of *evaluation* as a promising step in furthering the maker's purpose.

VII. The Elasticity of Process and Product

We began with the idea of process as underlying the understanding of products, and it is this idea we have been considering throughout. We must not, however, fall into the error of assuming that the educational importance of process is subsidiary to that of available products. Processes capable of aiding in the making of further works have intrinsic value; the justification for emphasizing them in education does not hinge solely on their contribution to an understanding of past works. It is our choice of theme, rather than a general criterion of value, that has singled out such contribution for special attention here.

In considering our theme, we have treated the ideas of process and product as relatively clear and durable notions. In fact, however, both notions are elastic and the boundary between them is hardly fixed. To emphasize what has hitherto been deemed process in a particular instance may in fact be to objectify it, thus relocating a familiar border between the two, and inviting a shift of attention, an opening of the mind to a new prospect of value. A child who first heeds the adage "It's not whether you win or lose, it's how you play the game" is going to perceive the game situation differently. New care will go into the style and ethic of play, new discrimination will be accorded the performance—hitherto regarded only as means, now to be seen as end or object in its own right.

The word "object" in fact carries both the connotation of end or goal, and that of actual thing. Performance singled out as object, in the sense of *end*, i.e., taken as a goal of action, is objectified in status, made an *object* in the sense of independent thing, or product. It can now be regarded, even by its author, as accessible from multiple perspectives, as having discoverable characteristics beyond his intention, as needing to meet independent standards. The development of a child's sportsmanship modifies his or her perception and alters responsibility, as does the birth of an ethical sense about the quality of one's actions as independent of their consequences. Cultural differences in attitudes toward the arts provide another illustration. By contrast with Western attitudes toward painting as products, to which the artists' activities are means, certain Eastern conceptions consider these activities themselves as *products,* taking the resultant paintings rather as *by-products*. Once having entertained such a reallocation of "object" status, one's perceptive attitudes have been altered significantly.

Even when the earlier notion of the product is retained, products are seen differently in light of the stress on originating performance. Thus, winning the game takes on an increment of value for one who has adopted the "how you play the game" morality. Hedged about by such morality, winning becomes a more difficult prize. A game won through the violation of sportsmanlike standards is now a devalued object, whereas a game lost retains a measure of value nonetheless, if such standards have been upheld. Moral value is in general ascribed on the basis of the quality of action rather than its success, such quality to be seen in the action itself—which is not merely a means to moral status but rather its proper locus. Similarly, the scientific character of an argument is to be found in its own quality rather than in the truth or falsity, or other feature, of the theory to which it leads. To come to view a scientific argument not merely as a means to an end but as a performance to be judged by independent standards is to acquire a new perception of scientific theories themselves.

VIII.   Process and Product Related

We have lately broadened the notions of process and reenactment to register the element of free play. But even these broader notions will not yield the result that reenactment of the maker's process is *sufficient* for an understanding of the product. For, as argued earlier, the product incorporates objective surprises, influences external to the maker's purposive activity, even taking free play into account. Furthermore, we have seen that reenacting the maker's process is not *necessary*, either, for an understanding of the product, which has, after all, its own life as an object. Nevertheless, grasping the maker's process at least tells us what he was *trying* to do. The purpose or goal of the making constitutes an operative standard against which he is prepared to judge the eventual product.

This standard is, of course, not immutable. Alertness to the product's threatened deviation from the expected outcome may lead the maker to alter the initial plan as well as—or instead of—reworking the product. But the possible later alteration of a plan does not diminish the fact that until such alteration occurs, it imposes order on action, defining presumptive success and setting criteria of relevance.

The question, however, is why *we* should be interested in reenacting the maker's teleological process. Certainly, from the maker's own point of view, his or her initiating purpose is important in the ways just outlined. But we are now trying to understand the product from *our* point of view, and the maker's position is not—for us—privileged. Standing where we do now, after the fact and outside the teleological process of the maker, we are not bound by his or her initiating purpose. We may discern features, functions, and potentials of the product far outside the range of the purpose that led to its making. Why then should we seek to reenact the maker's teleological process?

Such reenactment, I now suggest, allows us to *relate* process and product, to understand them in connection with one another and so to learn something valuable about action in general. It is true that process does not fully determine product, and it is therefore also true that understanding the product must have an interpretation independent of initiating process. But an understanding that is thus independent leaves out the important relation of the two—the fact that the product was brought about at least in part by the teleological process. It is this relation that makes criticism and evaluation possible for the maker in both the directions outlined above: the product that fails to fulfill initial plans may be further modified, or it may, rather, stimulate a revision of plans. Idea is tested by reality, reality is further altered by idea. To view the product in *relation* to its initiating process thus gives an insight into the evaluation of thought and action in general.

Indeed, that the product has unforeseeable features and unplanned consequences is not a fact in isolation, but must be brought into contact with the maker's initiating purposes. Otherwise, such purposes run along on their own tracks, unenlightened by experience, while experience leads on to prospects unaffected by thought. Once the relation in question is given primary emphasis, the notion of making is itself transformed, no longer seen as a single episode (like the Divine "Let there be light!" whereupon there was light), but rather as a course of experimental acts, probes, and reorientations by the maker in which purpose and outcome may be brought into closer coordination over time. The independent understanding of the product is not a stopping point for the intelligent maker. Rather, it is a recurring phase in the course of his or her creation, allowing continual monitoring and reevaluation in the light of purpose. The educational emphasis on process thus prompts us to see the product as both a *test* of, and *testable* by, the purpose that helped bring it into existence. Neither product nor purpose is self-enclosed and final.

Now it is true that, standing outside the teleological process of the particular maker, we are not bound by his or her initiating purpose. But through analysis of the product from the perspective of such purpose, we may exercise and improve upon our own capacities for critical understanding. Studying past chess games, works of art, scientific experiments, political decisions, or military encounters may thus improve the discrimination we bring to our own actions, without committing us in any way to the strategies employed in the cases under study. And improvement in the ways we ourselves act, the ways human beings in general translate their purposes into reality, is after all a fundamental goal of all reflective education.

IX. Traditions of Effort

The products central to education are, furthermore, not in fact isolated or idiosyncratic. It is not just formal lessons in intelligent action that we are afforded by studying the particular products enshrined in typical curricula—sharing such abstract lessons in critical thinking with the makers of these products, but not sharing their particular purposes. The products of human effort that are central to education are themselves organized by historic traditions and ideals that bind generations together. Viewed historically, processes of making comprise courses of experimental trials carried out by generations of individuals who share substantive purposes as well as formal patterns of intelligence. We resonate with the struggles of past scientists in the pursuit of an understanding of nature, for it is a pursuit we ourselves share. Such pursuit marks out an endless path of striving along which particular achievements are but landmarks to further effort by contemporary men and women. We are able not only to understand but also to sympathize with the experiments of artists in articulating fundamental discriminations and insights, taking joy in their successes as we continue the quest for further such articulations.

To view past works—whether of art, or science, or architecture, or music, or literature, or mathematics, or history, or religion, or philosophy—as given and unique objects rather than as incarnations of process is to close off the traditions of effort from which they emerged. It is to bring these traditions to a full stop. Viewing such works as embodiments of purpose, style, and form revivifies and extends the force of these traditions in the present, giving hope to creative impulses active now and in the future. To value such traditions requires an emphasis on process. Conversely, the strength of our emphasis on process is a measure of the values our education embodies. Appreciating the underlying process does not, by any means, exhaust the possibilities of understanding. But the understanding it does provide is a ground of further creativity in thought and action.

Notes

1. Henri Poincaré, "Mathematical Definitions and Education," in his *Science and Method* (New York: Dover, 1952), pp. 129–30. See also my "Basic Mathematical Skills," Chapter 7, below. I discussed Poincaré's views earlier, in Chapter 3 of my *Conditions of Knowledge* (Chicago: Scott, Foresman [now University of Chicago Press], 1965.

2. R. G. Collingwood, *The Idea of History* (New York: Oxford University Press, 1956), p. 215.

3. Moses Maimonides, *The Guide for the Perplexed,* trans. M. Friedländer (New York: Pardes, 1946), pt. 3, chap. 21, "The Creator's knowledge of his Production is Perfect," pp. 295ff.

4. In a letter to Max Born, Einstein wrote: "You believe in God playing dice and I in perfect laws in the world of things existing as real objects, which I try to grasp in a widely speculative way." See P. A. Schilpp, ed., *Albert Einstein: Philosopher-Scientist* (New York: Tudor, 1949), p. 176.

5. W. V. Quine, *Methods of Logic* (New York: Henry Holt, 1950), pp. 190–91.

6. Albert Einstein, "Autobiographical Notes," trans. P. A. Schilpp, in Schilpp, ed., *Albert Einstein: Philosopher-Scientist,* p. 7.

7. R. G. Collingwood, *The Principles of Art* (London: Oxford University Press, 1938), chaps. 1 and 2.

8. The notion of surprise is discussed in my "In Praise of the Cognitive Emotions," Chapter 1, above.

Part II

Symbolism

4

Educational Metaphors

If we compare metaphors with definitions and slogans, some contrasts are immediately apparent. Metaphors are not normally intended to express the meanings of terms used, either in standard or in stipulated ways. Rather, they point to what are conceived to be significant parallels, analogies, or similarities within the subject-matter of the discourse itself. Metaphorical statements often express significant and surprising truths, unlike stipulations, which express no truths at all, and unlike descriptive definitions, which normally fail to surprise. Although they frequently, like programmatic definitions, convey programs, metaphors do so always by suggesting some objective analogy, purporting to state truths discovered in the phenomena before us. Like slogans in being unsystematic and lacking a standard form of expression, they nevertheless have a much more serious theoretical role. They cannot generally be considered as mere fragments crystallizing the key attitudes of some social movement, or symbolizing explicit parent doctrines. Rather, they figure in serious theoretical statements themselves, as fundamental components.

The line, even in science, between serious theory and metaphor, is a thin one—if it can be drawn at all. To say "This table is composed of electrons" is clearly (at least) to invite comparison of the table and aggregates of tiny particles whose behavior is further elaborated in other statements. To be sure, the initial metaphor must lead to refinements in the comparison, expressed literally, and to experimental confirmation of predictions or other inferences derived from them. But the same holds true of theories generally, and there is no obvious point at which we must say, "Here the metaphors stop and the theories begin." In education, too, metaphorical statements are frequently found in key theoretical contexts as well as in policy contexts. What do they convey and how? We shall proceed from some general remarks to a consideration of selected educational metaphors.

Reprinted from Israel Scheffler, *The Language of Education* (Springfield, Ill.: Charles C. Thomas, 1960), pp. 47–59.

Generally, we may regard the metaphorical statement as indicating that there is an important analogy between two things, without saying explicitly in what the analogy consists. Now, every two things are analogous in some respect, but not every such respect is important. Still, the notion of importance varies with the situation: what is important in science may not be important in politics or art, for example. If a given metaphorical statement is to be judged worthwhile or apt, the analogy suggested must be important with respect to criteria relevant to the context of its utterance.

Further, the metaphorical statement does not actually state the analogy, even where a relevantly important one exists. It is rather in the nature of an invitation to search for one, and a metaphor is in part judged by how well such a search is rewarded. Again, the pattern is similar to that of a theory or, if you like, a theoretical hunch. It is no wonder, then, that metaphors have often been said to organize reflection and explanation in scientific and philosophical contexts. In practical contexts too, metaphors often serve, in a way analogous to programmatic definition, as ways of channeling action, although always by purporting to indicate that some important analogy may be found within the relevant subject-matter.

Aside from independent evaluation of programs that may be conveyed by particular metaphorical assertions, metaphors may be criticized in roughly two ways. First, we may reach the conclusion that a given metaphor is trivial or sterile, indicating analogies that are, in context, unimportant. Second, we may determine the limitations of a given metaphor, the points at which the analogies it indicates break down. Every metaphor is limited in this way, giving only a certain perspective on its subject, which may be supplemented by other perspectives. Such limitation is no more reason to reject a metaphor completely than the fact that alternative theories always exist is in itself a reason to reject any given theory in science. Nevertheless, a comparison of alternative metaphors may be as illuminating as a comparison of alternative theories, in indicating the many-faceted character of the subject. Such a comparison may also provide a fresh sense of the uniqueness of the subject, for to know in what ways something is like many different things is to know a good deal about what makes it distinctive, different from all the others. Lastly, where a particular metaphor is dominant, comparison helps in determining its limitations and in opening up fresh possibilities of thought and action. In the rest of this chapter, we shall be concerned to make such a comparison of common metaphorical ways of speaking about education.

Max Black suggests that the familiar growth metaphor is one that lends itself to the expression of revolt against educational authoritarianism.[1] How does this happen? There is an obvious analogy between the growing child and the growing plant, between the gardener and the teacher. In both cases, the developing organism goes through phases that are relatively independent of the efforts of gardener or teacher. In both cases, however, the development may be helped or hindered by these efforts. For both, the work of caring for such development would seem to depend on knowledge of the laws regulating the succession of phases. In neither case is the gardener or the teacher indispensable to the development of the organism, and, after they leave, the organism continues to mature. They are both concerned to help the organism flourish, to care for its welfare by providing optimum conditions for the operation of laws of nature. The growth metaphor in itself thus embodies a modest conception of the teacher's role, which is to study and then indirectly to help the development of the child, rather than to shape him into some preconceived form, a contrary metaphor that we shall presently consider.

Where does the growth metaphor break down? It does seem plausible with respect to certain aspects of the development of children, that is, the biological or constitutional aspects. Regarding these, we can pretty well say, roughly, what sequences of stages may be normally expected, and how the passage from stage to stage may be helped or hindered by deliberate effort on the part of others. Where such knowledge is lacking concerning details, it may presumably be furnished by further investigation. The nature and order of these stages of physical and temperamental development, and of the capacities for behavior they make possible, are, indeed, relatively independent of the action of other individuals, although even here cultural factors make their impact.

If we once ask, however, how these capacities are to be exercised, toward what the temperamental energy of the child is to be directed, what sorts of conduct and what types of sensitivity are to be fostered, we begin to see the limits of the growth metaphor. The sequence of physical and temperamental stages is, in fact, quite compatible with any number of conflicting answers to these questions. For these aspects of development, there are no independent sequences of stages pointing to a single state of maturity. That is why, with regard to these aspects, it makes no literal sense to say, "Let us develop all of the potentialities of every child." They conflict and so cannot all be developed. To develop some is to thwart others. To withdraw is not to allow nature's wisdom full scope, but to decide in one way rather than another, where both are compatible with nature; responsibility for such a decision cannot be evaded.

It has often been remarked that to think of history as if it were a plant, whose development through natural stages can only be facilitated or retarded by individuals, is a way of evading responsibility for affecting social events through choice and action.[2] It should be even more obvious that the course of children's social, cultural, and moral development is not divided into natural stages that cannot be fundamentally altered by others. It is clear that adults—parents and teachers—do more than simply facilitate the child's development toward a unique stage of cultural maturity.

It is the latter insight that underlies another familiar educational metaphor, that of shaping, forming, or molding. The child, in one variant of this metaphor, is clay, and the teacher imposes a fixed mold on this clay, shaping it to the specifications of the mold. The teacher's initiative, power, and responsibility are here brought into sharp focus. For the final shape of the clay is wholly a product of his choice of a given mold. There is no independent progression toward any given shape, as there is with respect to the growth of acorns, for example. Nor is there any mold to which the clay will not conform. The clay neither selects nor rejects any sequence of stages or any final shape for itself. The one choosing the mold is wholly responsible for the result.

In the light of our previous remarks on the growth metaphor, it is clear that this molding metaphor does not fit the biological-temperamental development of the child, which is not alterable throughout by adult action. The molding metaphor does, however, seem more appropriate than the growth metaphor as regards cultural, personal, and moral development, which is to a greater extent dependent on the character of the adult social environment.

But even here the molding metaphor has its limitations. In the case of the clay, the final shape is wholly a function of the mold chosen. The clay neither selects nor rejects any given mold. The clay is, further, homogeneous throughout, and thoroughly plastic. The shape of the mold is fixed before the molding process and remains constant throughout. Each of these points represents a dissimilarity with respect to teaching. For even if there are no laws of cultural, moral, and personal development, there are nevertheless limits imposed by the nature of the pupils upon the range of developments possible. These limits say what *cannot* be done with the material rather than what *will* develop. Human nature does not automatically select, but it rejects some forms that adults may choose for it. Further, these limits vary from student to student and from group to group. The student population is neither thoroughly homogeneous nor thoroughly plastic. Thus, if the educator's decisions are not made for him by nature, neither are they unlimited by nature, and a study of these limits may make his decisions wiser. Finally, if the teacher is indeed to pay attention to the nature of his students, he will modify his methods and aims in the course of his teaching and in response to the process itself. His teaching is, then, not comparable to a fixed mold, but rather to a plan modifiable by its own attempted execution.

It is the latter features of teaching that are accentuated in what may be called the art metaphor in any of several forms, for example, that relating to sculpture. The sculptor's statue does not grow of itself out of the rock, requiring only the artist's nurture; the artist exercises real choice in its production, yet his initial block of marble is not wholly receptive to any idea he may wish to impose on it. It rejects some of these by its internal structure. Neither is every block of marble like every other. Each block requires individual study of its individual capacities and limitations. Finally, the artist's initial idea is not one that is fully formed in advance, remaining fixed throughout. It gets the process started, but is ordinarily modified by the process itself, during which the artist is continually learning as well as creating.

This sculpture metaphor seems particularly apt with respect to the features just described, but it cannot be said that it is perfect, or even that it is better in every way than the ones previously considered. For example, the growth metaphor at least acknowledges the continuing development of the object in question after the departure of the gardener, whereas the sculpture metaphor does not; the statue ceases to grow when the sculptor is finished with it. Nor is the teacher, unlike the sculptor, bound only by aesthetic standards. His aims and methods are subject to moral and practical criticism as well.

Thus it seems mistaken to try to find a progressive order of metaphors in education, each metaphor more adequate and comprehensive than the last. Here the comparison of such metaphors with scientific theories itself breaks down. Educational metaphors in general use are of help in reflecting and organizing social thought and practice with respect to schooling, but they are not tied in with processes of experimental confirmation and prediction. They thus do not develop cumulatively as do scientific theoretical frameworks. They are rather to be thought of, perhaps, as ranged around their common subject, whose individual complex of features may be illuminated by a comparative examination of the metaphors.

The analogy indicated by a given metaphor may, as suggested earlier, be important in one context but not in another. A good metaphor is thus not generally good in every context. This fact is important for our present discussion, for education, as we have stressed, is the common ground of a variety of contexts. It is thus wise to be critical about accepting in a given context metaphors that have proved illuminating elsewhere, even though it is the same subject that is involved in both cases. The transplantation of metaphors may, indeed, be misleading inasmuch as it may blur distinctions vital in the new context though unimportant in the old.

The effects of such transplantation may be illustrated by reference to a widespread metaphorical account of education that is clearly related to the growth metaphor but is more inclusive; we will here call it the "organic metaphor." There are numerous variants and uses of this metaphor in educational writings; we shall here give a brief description for the purposes of discussion.[3] Culture, in the anthropological sense, in which it comprises the mores, folkways, technology, social organization, language, law, ideology, science, and art of a given society, is taken as analogous to life in the individual organism. Just as living things are different from inanimate things in maintaining themselves by renewal, in reacting to external forces so as to retain their equilibrium with the environment, using these forces as means of further growth, so cultures retain their continuity by reacting to external forces in such a way as to maintain their equilibrium and to grow adaptively and creatively. Although individual life ends with the death of the individual, cultural life does not. Just as the individual's several cells and tissues die and are replaced while his life goes on, so the culture's "cells"—that is, its individual members—die and are replaced without destroying the life of the culture. The cells in each case do not all die simultaneously but rather continuously, and they are continuously replaced. The processes by which new physical cells replace the old in the individual organism are responsible for preserving biological continuity. The processes by which new members of a culture replace the old guarantee cultural continuity. These latter processes constitute education, whose function is to transmit the culture's life from the group to each new member, thus renewing it continuously.

Now the organic metaphor, resting on the above analogies, assimilates education to the processes by which individuals take on the environing culture. There is real point in so doing in a variety of contexts. If we consider, in particular, anthropological or historical studies in which specific cultures are sometimes taken as units of investigation with a view toward determining their internal structures or the laws governing their structural changes, it may be desirable to group acculturating processes under a single rubric and to study their place in the "patterns of culture" as well as their mechanisms. In psychological investigations, too, where the attempt is made to discover cross-cultural laws of learning, it may be convenient to classify all processes of social learning under a single label as preliminary to this attempt. The organic metaphor in these contexts is perhaps helpful in comparing acculturating processes to regenerative processes in the biological organism. Like the latter, acculturating processes may be studied as relating to other phenomena, and as comprising a variety of mechanisms, whose laws need to be determined.

Nevertheless, when the organic metaphor is transplanted into practical contexts in which social policy is at stake, it may become positively misleading, since it makes no room for distinctions that are of the highest importance in practical issues. There are, for example, no moral distinctions among regenerative processes in the individual organism, whereas such distinctions, with respect to cultural "regenerative" processes, are often at the very center of social controversy. Such distinctions are expressed, for example, in the separation of teaching from force, propaganda, threat, and indoctrination. In addition, biological regenerative processes are not, in general, considered to be subject to choice and control, whereas social processes, to a significant extent, are. It is just where alternative choices are thought to be possible that issues of social policy take shape.

To compare the continuity of cultures to that of individual lives is, moreover, to oversimplify in the extreme. For individual continuity, there are fairly definite biological criteria and the range of variation consonant with continuity is fairly well given, for example, in descriptions of the life cycle. For cultures there are no similarly definite criteria, no known laws of growth or normal patterns of life cycle. We cannot readily say, in advance, how far a culture may change from its past character without losing its identity. Without specification of some standard of cultural continuity, it is thus not clear how education is construed when explained in terms of its contribution to such continuity. The continuity of any culture may be furthered in different, and conflicting ways, in accord with different standards of continuity that may be chosen. Such differences between standards are of moral, hence practical significance, although all such standards are compatible with talk of cultural continuity in the abstract.

When, further, the notion of "function" is transferred from biological to social contexts, an analogous indeterminacy results,[4] so that even with some specification of the respect in which cultural continuity is to be understood, to say that the function of education is to preserve cultural continuity is still inadequate. When we speak of the function of this or that biological mechanism, we speak, roughly, of its contribution to the normal or satisfactory working of the organism. For example, to say that the function of the heartbeat is to circulate blood round the body is to say that such blood circulation, which the heartbeat effects in usual circumstances, is indispensable to the normal working of the organism in question. Thus, also, to speak of the function of regenerative processes as the replacement of old cells with new ones is to say that the replacement resulting from the usual operation of such processes is indispensable to the normal working of the biological organism. In such cases, the concept of "normal working," is fairly clear.

If, however, we are to suppose that the cultural continuity allegedly effected by education is, similarly, indispensable to the normal or satisfactory working of the culture, we require, similarly, a clear notion of such working. Unfortunately, such a clear notion is lacking. Thus, waiving, for the moment, all questions concerning the interpretation of continuity, we still cannot claim that assertions about the function of education are clear in the sense in which "function" statements are clear in biology. We need, at the very least, to provide some independent specification of the standard of normal working that is being assumed.

Suppose, however, that such specification is supplied in a particular discourse that also specifies a special use of the term "continuity." In such a case, the assertion that the function of education is to preserve cultural continuity becomes analogous to biological "function" statements in point of clarity. Nevertheless, the moral distinctions that are uppermost in issues of educational and social policy contexts are omitted from the picture. What is worse, the positive moral connotation of the term "function" (which derives, perhaps, from its relation to biologically satisfactory working which is generally favored) suggests that the notion of social function also implies moral value.

It is obvious upon reflection, however, that no moral conclusions can be drawn from attributions of social function in the manner described, and, *a fortiori*, that positive evaluation is not implied. Suppose, for example, we specify, first, that by "continuity" we shall refer to the maintenance of continued attitudes of political and intellectual docility on the part of the population, and, second, that by "normal working" we shall refer to the unopposed rule of the current masters of a given dictatorship. We may now group together under the label "education" all those processes of suppression, deception, distortion, indoctrination, and threat by which political and intellectual docility is achieved, and we may conclude by declaring that the function of education in the society in question is to preserve its continuity. Given the two specifications mentioned, the assertion is clear and, moreover, true. For the docility resulting from the processes referred to is indeed indispensable to the tranquility of a dictatorship. It does not follow that such processes *ought* to be employed or approved. It does not follow, either, that dictatorships *ought* to work normally or satisfactorily in the specified sense, i.e., that they ought to be unopposed. The moral issues are not only not stressed in social "function" statements, but are often confused by the socially irrelevant connotation of value surrounding the term "function."

In the example just discussed, it is clear that a moralist might quarrel with the specification given of "normal working"; he might also propose a different use for "continuity." In this way, he might be able to retain the assertion that the function of education is to preserve continuity, but in a wholly different interpretation. Alternatively, he might abandon the "function" assertion to others, expressing his moral views instead by saying that the teacher has obligations that are independent of social continuity in various prevalent senses, namely, obligations to tell the truth, to respect the intelligence of the student, to earn his trust by being sincere and open in his dealings with him.

We may approach the general point we have here been emphasizing by a consideration of the notion of teaching, which is considerably narrower than that of acculturation. Every culture, we may say, normally gets newborn members to behave according to its norms, however these are specified, and many cultures have agencies devoted to this job. But not every way of getting someone to behave according to some norm is teaching. Some such ways are purely informal and indirect, operating largely by association and contact, as languages are normally learned. But not every formal and deliberate way is teaching, either. Behavior may be effectively brought into accord with norms through threats, hypnosis, bribery, drugs, lies, suggestion, and open force. Teaching may, to be sure, proceed by various methods, but some ways of getting people to do things are excluded from the standard range of the term "teaching." To teach, in the standard sense, is at some points at least to submit oneself to the understanding and independent judgment of the pupil, to his demand for reasons, to his sense of what constitutes an adequate explanation. To teach someone that such and such is the case is not merely to try to get him to believe it: deception, for example, is not a method or a mode of teaching. Teaching involves, further, that if we try to get the student to believe that such and such is the case, we try also to get him to believe it for reasons that, within the limits of his capacity to grasp, are *our* reasons. Teaching, in this way, requires us to reveal our reasons to the student and, by so doing, to submit them to his evaluation and criticism.

To teach someone, not that such and such is the case, but rather *how* to do something, normally involves showing him how (by description or examples) and not merely setting up conditions under which he will, in fact, be likely to learn how. To throw a child into the river is not, in itself, to teach him how to swim; to send one's daughter to dancing school is not, in itself, to teach her how to dance. Even to teach someone *to* do something (rather than how to do it) is not simply to try to get him to do it; it is also to make accessible to him, at some stage, our reasons and purposes in getting him to do it. To teach is thus, in the standard use of the term, to acknowledge the "reason" of the pupil, i.e., his demand for and judgment of reasons, even though such demands are not uniformly appropriate at every phase of the teaching interval.

The distinctions here discussed between teaching and fostering the acquisition of modes of behavior or belief are, we may say, distinctions of *manner*. They depend on the manner in which such acquisition is fostered. The organic metaphor, as we have seen, focuses on the continuity of the culture's life—in effect, on the behavioral norms and beliefs forming the *content* of the culture. It makes no distinctions in manner of acquisition of this content, of the sort we have illustrated by referring to the concept of "teaching." It is these distinctions, however, that are central to moral issues concerning social and educational policy. The usefulness of the organic metaphor in certain contexts cannot be taken to show that the distinctions of manner referred to are of no practical or moral movement, that, for example, teachers ought, by any means and above all, to adjust students to the prevailing culture (specified in any way you like) and to ensure its continuity (no matter how specified). Whether teachers ought or ought not to do just that or some alternative is an independent and serious moral question that requires explicit attention. That it receives no emphasis in the organic metaphor indicates not that the question is unimportant, but that this metaphor is inappropriate in practical contexts.

We shall end this discussion by trying to show how fundamental the question of manner is, and we shall refer here again to the concept of "teaching." We have already taken pains to indicate that the notion of teaching is considerably narrower than that of acculturation. The fact that every culture may be said to renew itself by getting newborn members to behave according to its norms emphatically does not mean that such renewal is everywhere a product of teaching in the standard sense we have discussed. To favor the widest diffusion of teaching as a mode and as a model of cultural renewal is, in fact, a significant social option of a fundamental kind, involving the widest possible extension of reasoned criticism to the culture itself.

That this option may, in particular societies, lead to great changes in fundamental norms, beliefs, and social institutions, with respect to the prevailing culture, is indeed possible, even highly likely. But such a consequence need not always follow. In particular, it is not likely to follow where the culture itself institutionalizes reasoned procedures in its basic spheres, where it welcomes the exercise of criticism and judgment, where, that is to say, it is democratic culture in the strongest sense. To support the widest diffusion of teaching as a model of cultural renewal is, in effect, to support something peculiarly consonant with the democratization of culture and something that poses a threat to cultures whose basic social norms are institutionally protected from criticism. Such support is thus consistent with the vision of a culture where understanding is not limited and where critical judgment of policy is not the institutionalized privilege of one class, where policy change is not perforce arbitrary and violent, but channeled through institutions operating by reasoned persuasion and freely given consent. Many, even most, social thinkers have shrunk before such a vision and argued that culture cannot long survive under democracy in this sense. Others have urged the fullest institutionalization of reasoned criticism, fully aware that such a course indeed threatens societies with rigid power divisions, but denying that all societies are therefore threatened and that *no* culture can survive if it rests on free criticism freely exchanged. The issue, in short, is not whether culture shall be renewed, but in what *manner* such renewal is to be institutionalized. It is this fundamental practical issue that must not be obscured in practical contexts by metaphors appropriate elsewhere.

Notes

1. M. Black, "Education as Art and Discipline," *Ethics* 54 (1944): 290, reprinted in I. Scheffler, *Philosophy and Education* (Boston: Allyn and Bacon, 1958, 1966).

2. See, in this connection, K. Popper, *The Open Society and its Enemies*, Third Edition, London: Routledge & Kegan Paul Ltd., 1957 (First edition, 1945) and K. Popper, *The Poverty of Historicism* (London: Routledge & Kegan Paul, 1957).

3. This description is suggested by J. Dewey, *Democracy and Education* (New York: The Macmillan Company, 1916), chap. 1. In summarizing the chapter, Dewey writes, for

example: "It is the very nature of life to strive to continue in being. Since this continuance can be secured only by constant renewals, life is a self-renewing process. What nutrition and reproduction are to physiological life, education is to social life" (p. 11). My purpose is, however, to point out the dangers of the organic metaphor, not to criticize Dewey's use of it in the chapter cited. (Passage cited with permission of the Macmillan Company.)

4. For a detailed analysis, to which my treatment is indebted, see C. G. Hempel, "The Logic of Functional Analysis," in L. Gross *Symposium on Sociological Theory* (Evanston, Ill.: Row Peterson and Company, 1959). The heartbeat example in the text derives from Hempel.

5

Ten Myths of Metaphor

Various myths surround the topic of metaphor. I here criticize ten such myths, hoping thereby to open the way to a better understanding of the topic.

1. The Myth of Falsehood

Only literal statements are true, according to this myth. All the rest distort and falsify. The poets (as Plato taught us) lie; only the scientists tell the truth. To describe an unreliable, cowardly, or sickly person as a weak reed is just to speak a falsehood, which becomes a truth through negation: obviously, the person referred to is not a weak reed.

But it is obvious that he is not a weak reed only if "weak reed" is taken literally, for it is, indeed, obvious that no person is literally a reed, weak or otherwise. And it is utterly trivial to say that a metaphorical statement, *taken literally,* may be false. Taken metaphorically, however, the statement may well be true: he is indeed a weak reed, and it is false to deny that he is. To be sure, metaphorical assertions are eligible for falsehood. But they are, no more than literal assertions, always false.

2. The Myth of Embellishment

If not always false, then metaphors are always, at any rate, cognitively contentless—so runs the present myth. Rhetorical adornments merely, meta-

This article appeared originally in *Communication and Cognition* 19, nos. 3/4 (1986): 389–94. It is reprinted from *Journal of Aesthetic Education* 22, 1 (Spring 1988): 45–50. An account of various theories of metaphor is given in my book *Beyond the Letter* (London: Routledge & Kegan Paul, 1979). Some passages in sections 3, 5, and 6 below are taken from my book. The notion of "mention-selection," referred to in section 10, is introduced and discussed in my book as well as in my "Four Questions of Fiction," *Poetics* 11 (1982): 279–84, reprinted as well in my *Inquiries* (Indianapolis, Ind.: Hackett, 1986). I thank Catherine Z. Elgin and V. A. Howard for critical comments on the present article.

phors can (and, for the sake of theoretical clarity, should) always be stripped away, allowing the bare literal truth to shine forth.

But what remains after the metaphor is removed from the statement "War is hell"? Eliminating the predicate leaves a bare grammatical subject, not even a full sentence, true or false. Presumably, what is intended here is not mere removal but translation, or replacement by a cognitive equivalent. It is, notoriously, no easy task to specify criteria for such replacement. But the more fundamental point is this: To concede that the metaphorical attribution *has* a cognitive equivalent is to admit that it possesses cognitive content, after all. It is, of course, not in any case true that metaphors with cognitive content always have literal equivalents.

3. The Myth of Emotivity

Metaphors are, according to this myth, emotive and not at all, or not primarily, cognitive. Whatever may be said of cognitive equivalents, metaphors surely have no emotive equivalents. It is their high emotivity that sets them apart from literal statements, making them irreplaceable.

But is "a sparkling intelligence" or "a pedestrian analysis" highly emotive? Is, indeed, the doctor's metaphorical "You face an uphill struggle for your life" more emotive than "The tests show that you have cancer"? Whatever criteria may be specified for the elusive property of emotivity, literal expressions, too, may have it in abundance, as witness "neutron bomb," "Chernobyl," "leukemia." Emotions develop in the most intimate connection with cognitions; feelings respond to things as apprehended and comprehended. Why should literal accounts of things be any less related to the emotive life than metaphorical accounts? Why should emotional response to things **cognized** be better expressed by metaphorical than literal reference to such things?

4. The Myth of Suggestiveness

Metaphorical statements are false or contentless, but at least they are distinctive in their suggestiveness, according to the present myth. Cognitively deficient themselves, they nevertheless stimulate associations of ideas which may terminate in useful truths.

Why literal statements are thought to be poorer than metaphorical ones in their suggestive capabilities is not explained by this myth. Associations of ideas, after all, occur in response to all sorts of verbal (let alone nonverbal) stimulation. They are even set off by pure nonsense, for example, Jabberwocky. Why are literal statements, in particular deficient?

What this myth overlooks is that metaphorical statements that initiate new classifications and categories do so not, as nonsense syllables stimulate, by adventitious means, but through their own novel assertive content. They may indeed begin as metaphorical hypotheses, but they often (and without change of content) end as acknowledged truths, their once startling attributions now congealed into new literal references. That the table is a swarm of atoms, that we live at the bottom of a sea of air, that the mind processes information or forms images—these are by now literal clichés, the same statements that started life as bold metaphors.

5. The Myth of Communication

Such examples refute the myth of metaphors as exclusively devices of communication. This myth supposes that the thought is fully available to the thinker in purely literal terms, but that its communication requires, or is facilitated by, the use of metaphors. Metaphor is the packaging of literal thoughts for transmission to others, but forms no part of these thoughts themselves.

What is thus denied is the patent fact that metaphor serves the seeker and not alone the transmitter of truth, that scientific theorizing, for example, thrives on metaphorical description put forth in an investigative spirit. The theorist typically does not know in advance the detailed basis of the metaphorical description he proposes, guessing that a certain deliberate crossing of categories may be found increasingly significant with further inquiry. The metaphor embodying this guess does not require a prior determination of such significance. On the contrary, the metaphorical description itself serves as an *invitation*, to its originator and to others, to develop its ramifications. Its challenge is not to receive a fully substantiated message, but to find or invent new and fruitful descriptions of nature.

6. The Myth of Ownership

The present myth supposes that the author of a metaphor has exclusive rights or privileged access to it. As an instrumental device of communication, it is wholly under the control of its creator, shaped exclusively by his intent. Interpretation of a metaphor requires, ultimately, appeal to such intent.

What is here left out of account, as already noted in the last section, is the exploratory or heuristic role of metaphor. What this role implies, in particular, is that the author of a metaphor has no special key to its import, no privileged access, no rights of ownership. In creating a metaphor, one may surprise oneself. The invitation presented by a metaphorical utterance may lead us to rethink old material in the light of new categorizations or to consider newly discovered phenomena in terms already available. Whether the task be to incorporate the novel or to reorganize the familiar, metaphor often serves as a probe for connections that may improve understanding or spark theoretical advance.

7. The Myth of Metaphorical Truth

This myth holds that there are two species of truth, the one literal, the other metaphorical. "The match flamed" is held to be true in a way quite different from that in which "His eyes flamed" may be true. Adherents of this myth are thus seduced into a fruitless hunt for the special characteristics of metaphorical as distinct from literal truth, yearning for an essential difference between poetic and scientific utterance.

That the above two sentences differ may be readily admitted. But that their difference is to be located in the duality of truth is dubious. For each sentence is true under the selfsame general condition: ". . ." is true if and only if. . . . Thus, "The match flamed" is true if and only if the match flamed and "His eyes flamed" is true if and only if his eyes indeed flamed. That the first "flamed" differs in its extension from the second is a fact about these two replicas in particular, not a fact about what it means for their respective sentences to be true. Nor, *a fortiori*, does it require the postulation of two species of truth.

8. The Myth of Constancy

This myth holds that once a metaphor, always a metaphor. Contrary to the view that the literal is primary and the metaphorical mere embellishment, the present myth declares the metaphorical to be primary, because every term in use has indeed a metaphorical lineage. All speech is thus declared to be metaphorical.

A consequence of this myth is that the notion of the literal is emptied of content; correlatively, the notion of metaphor, as contrasting category, loses its point. This consequence is, however, avoidable, and without denying the pervasiveness of metaphorical lineage: what needs only to be acknowledged is the historical dimension—the fact that the literal-metaphorical contrast is effective not absolutely but relatively to time.

Given two extensionally divergent replicas of a term, i.e., two tokens of a certain type at a given time, we deem the one metaphorical whose interpretation is typically, or optimally, guided by an understanding of the other, which we take as literal. A coextensive replica of this metaphorical expression occurring at a later time may quite properly, however, be judged to be literal. The term, construed as the type, has altered in its metaphorical status over time. The first description of an electronic device as a calculator was metaphorical; nowadays such a description is literal.

9. The Myth of Formula

How nice it would be to have a simple formula for decoding metaphorical expressions. The myth that there is such a formula is an old one, often criticized but never eliminated. Indeed, it is likely to gain a new life with the aid of current computer technology and associated models of the mind.

The fact is that metaphorical expressions are not coded. They have no recipes, nor can they be exhaustively enumerated in dictionaries or code books. Understanding a metaphor requires interpretation and investigation in context.

The most popular candidate for a formula to shortcut such interpretation and investigation is the concept of similarity. It is, however, a vacuous concept, there being too many similarities to choose from. Similarities abound wherever one looks, but few will support true metaphorical descriptions. On the other hand, to supplement the notion of similarity with that of importance (i.e., to seek important similarities) introduces an ineradicable contextual reference which cannot itself be compressed into a formula. Here inspection of the context, ingenuity, and wit are required to take up the slack. In place of an automatic read-out from a code book or the routine application of a formula, we have an interpretive process of search and discovery.

10. The Myth of Objectualism

Comparison of objects, as suggested in the foregoing references to similarity, is certainly involved in metaphorical description, but it is a myth to suppose that only comparison of objects is involved. According to this myth, one compares the objects denoted metaphorically by a term with those denoted literally by that term. For example, in "Men are wolves," "wolves" is metaphorically applied to men while literally denoting members of Canis Lupus. Abstracting the features common to both sets of objects, one interprets the metaphor as attributing certain of these features, e.g., fierceness, to the metaphorical referents.

This myth is misguided not only because comparison and abstraction are too broad, requiring restriction by what wants attention in context. The further point is that metaphor is not wholly objectual in outlook. Its routes of comparison are often circuitous, touching not only on the objects in question and their features, but also on various representations of these objects. That wolves are, it is said, rather more pacific than their familiar stereotype will allow does not disqualify "Men are wolves" as a metaphorical attribution of fierceness to men. It is the stereotype representing wolves rather than features of the wolves themselves that gives the clue to this attribution. Nor does "The boss is a dragon" lack all sense in consequence of the fact that "dragon" literally has no objects at all to denote. Again, representative stereotypes (in this case, dragon images, descriptions, models, and portrayals) come to the rescue. For the term "dragon" serves not only as a denoting unit that in fact denotes nothing, but also as a caption for dragon-mentions, which are in fact, as indicated, plentiful. Such *mention-selection* aids the understanding of metaphors. We live, after all, in a world of symbols as well as other objects. Our view of objects and our knowledge of their representations serve alike as resources for interpretation.

6

Symbol, Ritual, and Cognition

The present paper outlines some new approaches to symbolism inspired by the recent work of Nelson Goodman,[1] which, in its broad perspective on symbolic functions, may be considered a proper descendant of the pragmatism of Peirce, James, and Dewey. Incorporating a comprehensive analysis of reference embracing the arts as well as the sciences, the nonlinguistic as well as the linguistic, the literal and the metaphorical, Goodman's work challenges self-imposed philosophical restrictions to the scientific and the formal, thus returning to a more generous pragmatic view and opening the way to new investigations in all areas of symbolism.

My treatment of ritual, based on studies reported in my book *Inquiries*,[2] outlines multiple symbolic functions of ritual, including denotation, exemplification, and reenactment, all of which serve to mark out a structure of historical time, space, and community. In addition, patterns of ritual repetition bring performers' minds into regular contact with symbolized properties, thus influencing their concepts and sensibilities.

The focus on symbolic aspects is an act of abstraction. It must not be taken as denying the importance of the social functions of ritual, nor of the belief system which, in every case, provides its context and motivation. On the other hand, to abstract from such features in order to concentrate on the symbolism of rites draws special attention to their cognitive roles, that is, their roles in conceptualization and reference and, consequently, in shaping the mental sensibilities and habits of their participants.

The mere assignment of cognitive roles to ritual comes into conflict with its prevalent devaluation as a hindrance to spontaneous religious feeling. Thus, William James's *Varieties of Religious Experience* begins by dividing the religious domain into the institutional and the personal, proceeding thereafter "to ignore the institutional branch entirely." The sort of religion in which James is himself interested gives rise, as he says, to "personal not ritual acts, the individual transacts the business by himself alone, and the

---

*Presented at the Peirce International Congress, 1989.

ecclesiastical organization, with its priests and sacraments and other go-betweens, sinks to an altogether secondary place. The relation goes direct from heart to heart, from soul to soul, between man and his maker."[3] Assimilated by James to institutional machinery that slows or obstructs the free flow of religious sentiment, ritual is here mentioned only to be dismissed.

It is true that, where it has not been thus dismissed, ritual has been assigned not to feeling but to the contrasting realm of cognition—but with equally devaluing effects. For it has here been associated with myth, which is viewed as defective cognition, bad science, pathological belief. Whether a hindrance to religious emotion or an objectification of falsehood or illusion, ritual has not often been considered as serving properly cognitive functions.

Two recent thinkers may be considered as pioneers of the symbolic treatment I offer: Ernst Cassirer and Susanne Langer. Cassirer proposes to redress the devaluative attitudes described above, interpreting mythical thought, always associated with ritual, as a positive stage in the development of science. Resting on a unity of feeling that views nature as "one great society, the *society of life*," myth perceives *physiognomic* rather than objective features—structuring a "dramatic world—a world of actions, of forces, of conflicting powers. . . . Mythical perception is always impregnated with these emotional qualities." This world is the first stage in the development of human thought, in turn overcome by the "world of our sense perceptions," which is, in its turn, succeeded by the generalizing concepts peculiar to the scientific understanding of the physical world. None of Cassirer's three stages is "a mere illusion," science does not "extirpate [its predecessors] root and branch," although it must abstract from them in order to attain the objectivity required for its own function.[4]

Although Cassirer does indeed deny that myth constitutes "a mere mass of unorganized and confused ideas," and affirms its role in structuring a world from which our "empirical thought" has grown,[5] he sees its virtue to lie not in its own cognitive deliverances but in its giving way developmentally to an eventually maturing science. His defense of myth and ritual is limited by its underlying contrast of emotion and science, strengthening the dubious view that cognition is scientific or nothing and the equally dubious view that scientific cognition is devoid of emotion.

Langer, unlike Cassirer, separates ritual from myth, associating myth with fantasy and dream but relating ritual rather to religious feeling, which is "bound . . . to set occasions, when the god-symbol is brought forth and officially contemplated." At first, "an unconscious issue of feelings into shouting and prancing," the agitation evolves into "a habitual reaction . . . used to *demonstrate*, rather than to relieve, the feelings of individuals." The overt act has in this phase become a gesture—no longer a symptom of feeling but a symbol of it—denoting it and thus bringing it to mind. As an articulation of feelings, ritual produces "not a simple emotion but a complex permanent *attitude* . . . an emotional pattern, which governs all individual lives. . . . A rite regularly performed is the constant reiteration of sentiments toward 'first and last things'; it is not a free expression of emotions, but a disciplined rehearsal of 'right attitudes.' "[6]

Langer, more clearly than Cassirer, separates the display of feelings from their articulation. As gestures, rituals are for her primarily symbolic or referential, denoting rather than evincing feeling. The feelings they denote record "man's response [to] the basic facts of human existence" as expressed by the sacred life-symbols arising in myth. But, regularly repeated, the ritual reference to such responses in itself shapes attitudes and forms habitual dispositions.

Langer is certainly right, I believe, in emphasizing the formalization of ritual and its gestural, that is, its symbolic character. But her interpretation is too restricted both in its conception of the symbolic process itself and in its designation of the objects symbolized in ritual. For she thinks of the process as *denotation* strictly, and she conceives the objects to be uniformly *feelings*. Rituals may, however, symbolize anything, not just feelings; as Cassirer put it, "a dramatic world— a world of actions, of forces, of conflicting powers." And the process of symbolization need not be restricted to denotation but may encompass other forms of reference as well. Indeed, ritual is typically symbolic in several modes simultaneously, and gathers strength thereby. The oft-noted capacity of ritual to survive changes in doctrinal interpretation may stem just from being linked by diverse bonds of reference to objects. When one or more are cut, the others hold fast. In the remainder of this paper, I extend the symbolic interpretation of Cassirer and Langer, without relying on the division between emotion and cognition. In contrast to both these authors, I emphasize the varieties of symbolic function displayed by rituals, and require neither special emotive qualities nor peculiar emotive objects.

We have seen that Langer speaks of ritual acts as *denoting*, thus regarding denotation as going beyond mere verbal description. Goodman not only endorses this broadening of the notion, understanding it to comprehend pictorial, gestural, and other sorts of representation. In addition, he expands the idea of *reference*, so that it encompasses not merely denotation but also *exemplification* and *expression*. We shall see that rituals may, accordingly, be understood as engaged in exemplifying and expressing, in addition to denoting. But how are these two new functions themselves to be interpreted?

To begin with, exemplification is the relation *being a sample of*: it relates a thing to those of its properties to which it also refers. A tailor's swatch, as Goodman explains, "does not exemplify all its properties; it is a sample of color, weave, texture, and pattern, but not of size, shape, or absolute weight or value."[7] Expression he treats as implying metaphorical exemplification, that is, reference by an object to a property it metaphorically possesses. Thus a given painting may, at one and the same time, denote a man, literally exemplify certain hues or patterns, and express—that is, metaphorically exemplify—melancholy.

Not only words and pictures but also gestures may denote, exemplify, and express. Ritual gestures, in particular, may denote or represent historical events, or events thought to be historical; they may portray expected occurrences or hoped-for outcomes, they may denote or purport to denote persons, gods, or things. They may perform this role through bodily movement, after the manner of mime; they may also employ the voice in song or speech. The range of ritual gestures indeed comprehends verbal gestures; thus, any denotative role that can be fulfilled by verbal means is also within the scope of ritual reference. Objects employed in ritual may also stand for, or refer, in a wide variety of ways.

Although not every ritual gesture denotes, every such gesture typically has specifications or prescriptions that it must satisfy. These may be transmitted orally or written down or understood in context, but that there is a right and a wrong way of execution is normally evident. It is this fact that constitutes the formalization of ritual gestures emphasized by Langer, who describes them as "bound to an often meticulously exact repetition, which gradually makes their forms as familiar as words or tunes."[8] What Cassirer says of sacrificial services may be considerably generalized: "The . . . service is fixed by very definite objective rules, a set sequence of words and acts which must be carefully observed if the sacrifice is not to fail in its purpose."[9] Now a proper performance of a rite often functions as a sample of it, that is, it literally exemplifies it. In this way, it lends itself to auxiliary use as a demonstration in the process of teaching the rite to learners. Rituals may thus be passed on, through participation which both satisfies their normative requirements and educates people in their use.

We have seen that Goodman treats expression as implying metaphorical exemplification. A picture may exemplify not only a certain style or pattern but also a certain feeling or movement, possessing the style or pattern literally, the feeling or movement metaphorically, but in both cases constituting a sample of, and referring to, the property possessed. A rite expressing a certain feature may, analogously, be taken as metaphorically possessing it and also referring to it. Particular rituals may thus be interpreted as expressing a wide range of features—for example, joy or sorrow, triumph or grief, elation or trust, yearning, contrition, or exaltation. The multiply symbolic character of ritual should here be recalled. Whatever a given rite may in fact denote, it may simultaneously exemplify, literally or metaphorically, quite different things. Explicitly representing episodes of a sacred story, it may at the same time express, rather than represent, dependence or victory, atonement or thirst for redemption.

The symbol expressing a feature must possess it. Must the user or producer or viewer of the symbol also possess it? Not so. "The properties a symbol expresses are its own property," writes Goodman. "That the actor was despondent, the artist high, the spectator gloomy or nostalgic or euphoric, the subject inanimate, does not determine whether the face or picture is sad or not. The cheering face of the hypocrite expresses solicitude, and the stolid painter's picture of boulders may express agitation."[10] Similarly, the feelings, thoughts, or other mental states of performers or spectators of a rite are to be distinguished from the features expressed by the rite itself.

Yet we here confront a striking contrast between arts and rites, ritual presenting a radically different aspect. For rituals are, in religious as distinct from magical contexts, typically intended to penetrate to the heart. Performers of rites are not actors. The question "Does he truly believe what he is saying?" is relevant to the ritual performer alone, while artful simulation of belief is a feat valued only in the actor. Although both actors and performers of religious ritual may indeed perform flawlessly while their thoughts and feelings are remote from the features expressed, a major point of ritual, although not of drama, is to affect the thoughts and feelings of participants, in part through repeated exposure to such features. We have seen Langer's emphasis on ritual repetition. Unlike a dramatic performance, a religious ritual usually has a characteristic pattern of recurrence; it is to be repeated with the seasons, or with other units of time, or with the important junctures of a life. Such regular recurrence functions to pattern the sensibilities of participants, in good part by repeated contact with features denoted, literally exemplified, or expressed.

True, not every expressed feature is, even theoretically, to be paralleled in the participant, in ritual as in art. For example, a rite expressing majesty may rather be hoped to induce faith or trust. And even where parallel features are indeed hoped for, successful execution of a rite on any given occasion does not hinge on satisfaction of this hope; that a participant's state of mind is incongruous with the expressed theme of the rite may lower its quality but does not, in general, argue that the rite has not taken place. Yet quality may indeed be affected, and this is a significant point: there is, in the case of ritual, a certain expected linkage between expressed properties and participants' mentality and sensibility; the cognition of expressed features, reinforced by repeated performance, is a major medium of such linkage. Regular recurrence is not only, as suggested by Cassirer and Langer, a force for the stylization of ritual acts; it is a way of strengthening their influence on the mind.

The ideal ritual participant is one whose own character is suitably affected by the role he performs and not simply one who skillfully conveys the character defined by his role. Although in drama the cheering face of the hypocrite may, as Goodman says, express solicitude, hypocrisy being irrelevant, it is absurd to suppose that hypocrisy is irrelevant to performance of a religious rite expressive, say, of contrition or repentance. Although in both cases hypocrisy is independent of what is expressed by the performance, it is only in the ritual case relevant to understanding the whole pattern of associated performances, functioning as it does to reduce hypocrisy in the participants themselves.

I have emphasized the importance of ritual recurrence in forcefully calling to mind those properties the rite denotes, exemplifies, or expresses. But this is not the whole story, for rituals, as R. S. Peters has remarked, "help to unite the past with the future and to convey the sense of participation in a shared form of life." They comprise not merely repeated action patterns but traditions, conveying, beyond each repetition of a performance, some sense of the fact that it *is* a repetition, some awareness of its predecessors. And such awareness I interpret in terms of an additional mode of symbolization that I call "reenactment."

I reserve the notion of *reenactment* for the relation between a ritual performance and its preceding ritual replicas, rather than using it, as is sometimes customary, for the relation between a performance and the event it commemorates. "Reenactment," in my usage, is a reproduction of the act, a co-exemplification of the same rite. Commemorated events, on the other hand, are typically denoted, represented, or portrayed rather than reproduced in ritual, even though the ritual aim may be to promote spiritual union with the historical agents in question. Even mimetic gestures do not, in general, reproduce the mimed activity; they exemplify some of its features, but not the activity itself, although they may vividly call it to mind. On the other hand, a performance that replicates earlier performances of a given rite reproduces them in constituting a sample of—exemplifying—the self-same rite.

In thus reproducing its earlier ritual replicas, each ritual performance refers indirectly to them, alludes to them, that is, while independently denoting whatever it may denote, and symbolizing in the other modes so far distinguished. In the regular recurrence of a rite, a sense thus builds up, in each new performance, of the prior performances to which it is ritually kin. The performance thus calls to mind not only the event that may be commemorated, but also the sequence of vehicles of its commemoration.

The relation of one performance to a replica is a relation holding between performances denoted by, and exemplifying, the same ritual specifications. The allusion by a present performance to earlier replicas may be thought of as transmitted through a two-link chain of exemplification as follows: the present performance is linked to the ritual specification it exemplifies, and this specification is in turn linked to past performances exemplifying it.

It is worth noting that such chains, widely available, become referentially operative only in certain cases. Thus, reenactment plays virtually no role in the arts, by comparison with religious ritual. A given performance of a musical work typically makes no reference to the past performances of the same work, although it may single out special performances as landmarks for comparison. By contrast, a ritual performance alludes to its own past kin, fostering in participants a sense of reenacting an important procedure. The relevant chain is referentially activated, and such activation is one symptom of the religious consciousness.

The marking out of ritually commemorated events helps to define a temporal matrix, and reenactment elaborates it further by articulating an ever-expanding ritual tradition. Concomitantly, reenactment serves also to form a conception of community. For the performers of past ritual replicas constitute a body of actors to which present performers relate themselves through reenactment and, hence, indirectly to one another. The community thus defined bears not only common bonds to the past but also common orientations in the present and outlooks for the future. Thus, an organization of time, as well as of the space occupied by a historical community, is facilitated.

This is perhaps the root of the emphasis on stabilization in primitive religion, in the work of Bergson, Cassirer, and others. In this vein Cassirer writes, agreeing with Bergson, "primitive religion can . . . leave no room for any freedom of individual thought. It prescribes its fixed, rigid, inviolable rules not only for every human action but also for every human feeling."[11] But as I have pictured it, the general phenomenon of ritual is no mere squelching of emotion, no cage of the feelings. Rather, we have to do with a cognitive ordering of categories of time, space, action, and community.

Notes

1. Nelson Goodman, *Languages of Art* (Indianapolis, Ind.: Hackett, 1976).
2. Israel Scheffler, *Inquiries* (Indianapolis, Ind.: Hackett, 1986).
3. William James, *The Varieties of Religious Experience* (New York: Random House, 1902, 1929), p. 30.
4. Ernst Cassirer, *An Essay on Man* (New Haven, Conn.: Yale University Press, 1944), pp. 76–83.
5. Ibid., p. 76.
6. Susanne K. Langer, *Philosophy in a New Key* (New York: Penguin Books, 1942, 1948), pp. 122–24.
7. Goodman, *Languages of Art*, p. 53.
8. Langer, *Philosophy in a New Key*.
9. Cassirer, *An Essay on Man*, p. 221.
10. Goodman, *Languages of Art*, pp. 85–86.
11. Cassirer, *An Essay on Man*, p. 225.

Part III
Curriculum

7

Basic Mathematical Skills

Familiarity—in life—may breed contempt. In thought, it typically breeds complacency and misunderstanding. The very familiarity of educational concepts often masks critical features of the problems facing us, lulling us all the while into a false sense of clarity and the fitness of things.

Thus we divide the matter of education into familiar "subject" categories and think thereby to have simplified and clarified the tasks of teaching. The subjects are, after all, drawn directly from parent disciplines, each with its distinctive and authoritative purchase on the world, each with its characteristic methodology and set of truths. Every subject is intellectually homogeneous within, and separable from every other without. Subjects are for the knowing, and knowing them is a matter of mastering their respective stores of truth and acquiring the respective methodologies from which their truths have sprung. Mastery of truths has to do with getting the appropriate beliefs; acquisition of methods and operations involves getting the right skills. For each subject there are characteristic and peculiar truths as well as distinctive and appropriate skills. To find these and to state them is to produce a curriculum. What could be more familiar—or more misguided?

Subjects are not, in fact, drawn directly or readily from their parent studies, and parent studies are not all disciplines.[1] (Is social science a discipline? Is the study of English language and literature? Is history?) Neither adult studies nor school subjects are written in the sky. The former are arranged for the expedient advancement of investigations and researches, the latter for the facilitation of learning and teaching in particular contexts—purposes that generate independent and powerful constraints. Neither studies nor subjects are internally homogeneous, nor are they wholly discrete. Their aims, structures, methods, and boundaries change over time, and there are overlappings and branchings of various sorts at any given time. The current

---

Presented at the Euclid Conference on Basic Mathematical Skills and Learning, sponsored by the National Institute of Education, October 1975. Reprinted from *Teachers College Record* 78, no. 2 (1976): 205–12.

"foreign relations" of subject areas (generally of little interest to the specialist) are, moreover, of particular concern to the educator, interested as he must be both in economizing educational effort and in broadening the student's intellectual and cultural perspectives.[2]

Nor is the concept of *knowing*—taken as comprising acquisition of the distinctive beliefs of a subject and its distinctive methods—anywhere near as complex enough to explicate the tasks of curriculum formation.[3] The aims of education must encompass also the formation of habits of judgment and the development of character, the elevation of standards, the facilitation of understanding, the development of taste and discrimination, the stimulation of curiosity and wonder, the fostering of style and a sense of beauty, the growth of a thirst for new ideas and visions of the yet unknown. The articulated truths and methods of a subject are raw materials; they have no fixed locus in the curriculum. They are given special forms of life by the curriculum design that puts them to use for educative purposes.

Finally, it is (to say the least) gratuitous to suppose that *methods* and *skills* are exactly correlated; the classification of methods is typically a "logical," epistemological, or normative matter, while the classification of skills is often a matter of the psychology of learning or cognition. There is no reason to suppose that methods or operations, as catalogued by disciplinary or subject specialists, are identifiable with skills, as conceived by psychologists of cognition. Nor is there any substance to the notion that there must be simple rules for translating methods or operations into underlying psychological processes. The word "skills," it is true, is ambiguous and is often used interchangeably with "operations" or with "methods," or used to refer to what is classifiable by appeal to the latter as, e.g., "capacities to perform such and such operations or to apply such and such methods." The skills of a subject, in the latter sense, are trivially derivable from a knowledge of its ingredient methods and operations. It is, however, fallacious to pass from the latter sense of the word to the sense in which "skills" refers to the basic processes of learning or cognition involved in applying a method or performing an operation. For the educator, this fallacy is a significant hazard: he must be concerned both with the intellectual methods of the subjects and with the psychological processes engaged in learning and applying them.

The Meaning of "Basic"

Let us direct some of the above reflections to the case of basic mathematical skills. The very phrase is difficult for a variety of reasons. I have suggested an ambiguity in the term "skills" as between "operations or methods" and "processes of learning or cognition." Consider now the force of the term "basic": does the phrase refer to skills important (perhaps necessary) for mathematics, to skills peculiar to mathematics, or to both? These senses diverge. The ability to follow an argument, for example, is certainly necessary for mathematics. But surely it is not peculiar to mathematics.

Take, then, the specific ability to follow a *mathematical* argument: is *it* not both important and peculiar to mathematics? The idea suggests, if it does not imply, that mathematics is internally homogeneous as to the argumentation it displays—a point to be considered in the next section. Moreover, the idea begs the critical question as to whether the ability to follow a mathematical argument—no matter how such argument may be characterized—is a separable skill from a psychological and educational point of view. Is it, indeed, optimally developed in isolation from nonmathematical materials, and is its sphere of exercise limited to the mathematical domain? If, in short, mathematical argument is peculiar to mathematics, it does not follow that the ability to learn, follow, or apply mathematical argument is peculiar to mathematics.

Furthermore, recent neuropsychological studies have cast empirical doubt on the correlation of subjects with mental processes. Such studies have tended to destroy the *a priori* skill-clustering fostered by traditional subject divisions: certain symbol-processing abilities appear to cut across these divisions in various ways, while other inherited rubrics appear to require new divisions.[4] It is conceivable to me that very many (possibly all) of the psychologically significant skills important for mathematics may be important outside mathematics, that the particular perceptual, symbolic, inferential, mnemonic, questioning,[5] strategic, and imaginative capacities exercised in mathematics are also exercised outside it. It seems to me, moreover, overwhelmingly likely that successful performance in mathematics rests not only on general skills but also on general attitudes and traits such as perseverence, self-confidence, willingness to try out a hunch, appreciation for exactness, and still others.

The Scope of "Mathematical"

Consider now the adjective "mathematical" in the phrase "basic mathematical skills." I have suggested that fundamental psychological processes connect mathematics with other fields of study. Here I argue that the subject itself is not all of a piece. Further, I conjecture that the oversimplified educational concept of a "subject" merges with the false public image of mathematics to form a quite misleading conception for the purposes of education: since it is a subject, runs the myth, it must be homogeneous, and in what way homogeneous? Exact, mechanical, numerical, and precise—yielding for every question a decisive and unique answer in accordance with an effective routine. It is no wonder that this conception isolates mathematics from other subjects, since what is here described is not so much a form of thinking as a substitute for thinking. What is in point is the process of calculation or computation, the deployment of a set routine with no room for ingenuity or flair, no place for guesswork or surprise, no chance for discovery, no need for the human being in fact.

Now calculation is certainly indispensable to mathematics, but it is not mathematics. When children are for the first time brought beyond the sphere of elementary calculation to the stage of problem-solving (perhaps in geometry), they naturally bring with them the impression that they are still learning the same subject. Yet here there are no routines for getting the right answer, here trial and error reign and there is ample scope for invention and surprise. The great gulf between mere calculation and problem-solving occurs within the subject, not beyond it. The tasks that are set, the purposes envisaged, the rules and constraints of the game are of a fundamentally different quality and are likely to evoke different applications and combinations of mental capacity. The notion of skill is thus in general not self-sufficient; it cannot eliminate needed reference to the nature of the tasks in question, their governing purposes and expected styles of execution.

The division I have just discussed, between computation and problem-solving, is a division internal to the school subject of mathematics. To elaborate it in teaching would help (I believe) not only to improve the process, but also to break down the mechanical stereotype of mathematics and relate the subject to other areas of creative thought. Other internal divisions are suggested by recent psychological studies, but are not as yet well understood. Certain sorts of injury to the brain may, for example, destroy the capacity to read while leaving intact the ability to recognize pictures, although both capacities are visual.[6] To what extent does success in geometry depend upon pictorial, as distinct from linguistic, processing capacities? In what ways indeed is a diagram like, and unlike, a picture? A map? An equation? A word description?[7]

Both the division between computation and problem-solving and the possible division between geometry and other branches of the subject are threatened by the popular conception of deduction. This conception deserves comment, for it offers the public a seemingly general way to override the two distinctions and assimilate mathematics once again as a species of mechanism. For consider an ordered list of statements comprising a deductive proof: each statement is an axiom or follows by a single application of a stated rule from earlier statements. The chain is held together by necessity, the strongest conceptual glue: if the premises be true, the conclusion cannot fail of truth. Where is there any looseness or leeway? The whole is tightly made, an army of statements marching in order by command, a machine whose gears mesh inexorably according to fixed structural patterns. How can there be any mention of trial and error, of discovery and surprise, in the same breath with deduction?

The flaw in this example is that the proof is *given* at the outset. Although each of its statements "follows" by rule, the proof is not generated by rule. The determination of its character as a proof may indeed be made by mechanical routine. It does not follow that such routines exist for the construction of proofs. Indeed, it is demonstrable that no such routines are generally available. To *find* a proof is no merely mechanical matter, but an open and creative challenge in which ingenuity and good fortune, trial and error, and—at best—heuristic maxims hold sway.[8]

Moreover, the use of any formalism requires intelligence in application. The problematic material to which it is applied must, ordinarily, undergo suitable preparation, a phase of "words into symbols" that is not itself governed by mechanical rules but rather by good sense and an intuitive grasp of the problem's context and description.[9] One can impeccably run through a formal routine stupidly applied; the cure for stupidity is, furthermore, not formal. The application of formalisms and problem-solving strategies takes place always in a context and for a purpose. Intelligent deployment in context requires not only proper management of the formalism but appropriate application; and the latter involves accurate observation, sensible reading, logical analysis of problematic statements, translation into appropriate symbolic form, and eventual translation back to suitable statements—all such tasks belonging to mathematical applications but also to virtually all other spheres of human thought.

Comprehension and Skill

I have said much about skill, virtually nothing about comprehension. What sort of skill is *that*? Elsewhere I have argued that it is not a skill at all.[10] To approach education as if it were always a matter of equipping the pupil with skills distorts our thinking. The category of skills has special features; these cannot be transported just anywhere.

A skill is capable of repeated exercise in separate episodes of performance, whereas comprehension is not thus exercised in performance. One who knows how to swim may swim every Thursday at 4:00 P.M.; can we say, comparably, that one who knows how to understand quantum theory understands it every Thursday at 4:00 P.M.? A skilled person may decide not to exercise his skill; a man who can play tennis may choose not to. A person with an understanding of quantum theory cannot, however, choose not to understand it. Nor can one speak of practice in the realm of comprehension as one does in reference to skills. One cannot develop an understanding of quantum theory by understanding it over and over again, nor can one deepen one's understanding by faithfully repeated performances of understanding. One can tell a pupil to practice writing out a proof; it makes no sense to tell him to practice understanding it.

If comprehension is not a skill, what is it then? Can understanding a proof be merely a matter of checking its demonstrative character? Such a check would yield the conclusion that what purports to be a proof really is one. Would it guarantee an understanding of the proof? If the answer is negative, the question is: What else could possibly be required as a condition of understanding?

The point is elusive, but I suggest that it has to do with appreciating the generality of the reasons behind each step.[11] These reasons are, further, of roughly two sorts:

(a) Deductive: Those that characterize a given line as axiomatic or else derivable, by a single application of a stated rule, from earlier lines. Comprehension here requires an appreciation of the generality of the rule, an ability to recognize analogous cases and to apply it elsewhere.

(b) Strategic: Those that characterize a given line as a promising step, in virtue of a certain strategic principle, toward the desired theorem. Comprehension here requires an appreciation of the general strategic principle, and it is also evinced in the treatment of parallel cases.

It is perhaps not misleading to describe deductive reasons as looking backward while strategic reasons look forward. Strategic reasons enable us, not to judge the *validity of the product,* but rather the *rationale of its step-by-step construction,* thus to enter into the mind of the maker. They answer the questions that are often so puzzling to the student: How did the author of the proof think to apply such and such rule to get the next line? Granted, the step is valid, but where in the world did he get the idea to take that step in the first place, and what made him think that it would bring him nearer the desired conclusion? To such questions, it is no answer at all to be told that the step is valid. And, without an appropriate answer, one can hardly be said to understand the proof in the full sense of the word. A student who blames himself for failure to understand may (I suggest) never have been helped to see the special character of his questions, and the special nature of strategic—as distinct from deductive—reasons. Poincaré speaks of the matter in terms of intuition and image, describing the needed insight as "seeing the end from afar."[12] I have elsewhere described it as a matter akin to grasping the author's *motive,* the embodiment of which is his strategy: what did he hope to achieve by this step and how is such achievement related to his final goal?[13]

Understanding is not a skill but rather a state—an attainment—which incorporates general capacities among its constituents. It constitutes a fundamental and important aim of education, because it places the particular item in a general framework of rules and principles. It not only gives evidence of the pupil's right to be sure of his particular items and, hence, of his knowledge of them. It reaches out from these items to whole infinities of parallel cases in which evaluations are to be made, and, moreover, new efforts undertaken. Nor is it an all-or-nothing affair, since it may grow gradually with the attempt to see how to deal with new cases. The very process of testing for understanding tends to develop it by forcing accommodation of the particular case with general principles.[14] The more reflective a grasp the pupil has of such principles and the more adequate they are to available cases, the less arbitrary the cases look and the more reasonable the principles—*and* the more adequate, moreover, the pupil's orientation to new problems he may confront.

Problems and Research

As suggested throughout the previous discussion, there is, I believe, much basic research to be undertaken, both of an analytical and of an empirical sort. There are also important studies to be conducted of a clinical and a practical kind. I shall comment briefly on these varieties.

As I have shown earlier, the familiar categories in which educational thinking is cast are replete with difficulties. These difficulties are conceptual, but they critically affect the organization of practice as well. Analytical study of educational concepts needs to be undertaken, with particular reference to their mathematical applications.

The materials of mathematics need to be studied, both in relation to the educational analyses just proposed and independently. I hope that the foregoing discussion has suggested the importance of the logical, or normative, analysis of mathematical operations and methods, as helping to set the aims of mathematical education. Such analysis should investigate the diversity of tasks and purposes embodied in the several areas of mathematics. The study of methods ought also be brought into connection with fields other than mathematics to discover new relations of a logical and epistemological sort.

Neither form of analytical study proposed is, of course, self-sufficient. Both need to be brought into communication with empirical considerations and inquiries of various kinds. I have mentioned some recent neuropsychological investigations into cognitive processes and the new articulations of skills and capacities to which they lead. Such studies, turned to the special concerns of mathematics, may well result in new pedagogical ideas of importance.

The study of so-called "disabilities" in reading and other language functions is one mode of access to an understanding of underlying processes. Analogously, the systematic study of "disabilities" and deficiencies in mathematical areas may reveal new insights into forms and limitations of comprehension, with pedagogical reverberations and suggestions for improvement. I suggest a large series of studies of deficiency of all sorts, including investigations into mathematical "trauma," illiteracy, and misunderstanding in children and adults.

The relation of psychological studies of mental process to normative studies of mathematical method needs to be systematically investigated. The relation should, moreover, also be set in the context of general aims of education. For mathematics, as I have earlier argued, is not an island: its linkages with all other areas of education need to be taken seriously, and studied systematically.

I have stated some conjectures about popular conceptions of mathematics and mathematical operations. All education is affected by prevailing attitudes and images concerning the content taught.[15] Studies of public attitudes toward mathematics might, it seems to me, reveal the sources of many difficulties, and perhaps point the way to some remedies.

Finally, I urge the study of teaching practice. What are the successful practices of good teachers? Why do they work? What skills do they embody? Such study ought to have a historical and comparative side and not restrict itself to local current custom.[16] But many good teachers now at work are no doubt doing good things capable of generalization. They are, however, unknown, and generally cannot inform others of their work through publication. They should be sought out and studied. Furthermore, teachers should be encouraged to develop new practices, and educators to design new patterns of teaching. I am persuaded that the intuitive practice of teachers is an important—perhaps the single most important—source of new notions for the improvement of practice and even for theoretical ideas.

The proposals for study here put forth require collaborative effort. Such collaboration is a difficult but crucially important element in any program for advancing our knowledge and practice in education. Mathematicians, teachers, psychologists, philosophers, social scientists, educational theorists, and others need to find appropriate channels for sharing ideas and learning from one another. To develop such channels would be a contribution of great importance.

Notes

1. On the notion of "discipline," see Israel Scheffler, *Reason and Teaching* (Indianapolis, Ind.: Bobbs-Merrill, 1973), chap. 4, pp. 45–57.

2. Ibid., p. 89.

3. On this point, see Israel Scheffler, *Conditions of Knowledge* (Chicago: Scott, Foresman, 1965), pp. 106–7.

4. See Howard Gardner, "A Psychological Investigation of Nelson Goodman's Theory of Symbols," *The Monist* 58, no. 2 (April 1974): 318–26; Nelson Goodman, "On Reconceiving Cognition," ibid., pp. 339–42; and H. Gardner, V. Howard, and D. Perkins, "Symbol Systems: A Philosophical, Psychological, and Educational Investigation," in *Yearbook of*

the National Society for the Study of Education, ed. D. Olson (Chicago: University of Chicago Press, 1974).

5. Cf. the emphasis on questions and the posing of problems by Stephen Brown and Marion Walter. When referring to problem-solving in this paper, I mean to include also the phase of problem-formulation stressed by Brown and Walter.

6. Gardner, "A Psychological Investigation of Nelson Goodman's Theory of Symbols," p. 324.

7. On these questions, see Nelson Goodman, *Languages of Art* (Indianapolis, Ind.: Bobbs-Merrill, 1968).

8. See, for the demonstration, A. Church, "A Note on the Entscheidungsproblem," *Journal of Symbolic Logic* 1 (1936): 40–41 and 101–2; and B. Rosser, "An Informal Exposition of Proofs of Gödel's Theorems and Church's Theorem," *Journal of Symbolic Logic* 4 (1939): 53–60. For general remarks, see W.V.O. Quine, *Methods of Logic* (New York: Henry Holt, 1950), pp. 190–91; and the entry by Alonzo Church, "Logic, Formal," in D. D. Runes, *Dictionary of Philosophy* (New York: Philosophical Library, 1942), pp. 170ff, esp. pp. 172 and 175.

9. See the section "Words into Symbols," in Quine, *Methods of Logic,* pp. 39–46.

10. See Scheffler, *Conditions of Knowledge,* pp. 17–21.

11. For a related discussion, see Scheffler, *Conditions of Knowledge,* pp. 70ff.

12. Henri Poincaré, "Mathematical Definitions and Education," in idem, *Science and Method,* trans. Francis Maitland (New York: Dover Publications, 1952), pp. 117–42, esp. pp. 129–30.

13. Scheffler, *Conditions of Knowledge,* p. 73.

14. Ibid.

15. See L. J. Cronbach and P. Suppes, eds., *Research for Tomorrow's Schools* (London: Collier, 1969), pp. 125ff.

16. Why, e.g., did Poland produce such a dazzling array of logicians between the World Wars?

8

Computers at School?

Introduction

In an essay published a little over twenty years ago, I described American education as then in the throes of a return to formalism. What I referred to was that period's renewed emphasis on academic values, and the rejection of earlier concerns with the child's growth as center of the educational process. The return to formalism also involved what I described as a

> vast . . . emphasis on educational technology, the development of devices, programs, and new curricula for the more efficient packaging and distribution of knowledge. What [had been], in the days of progressivism, a broad concern for scientific inquiry into processes of growth, perception, and socialization [had], in the name of hardheaded research and development, become more and more a preoccupation with the hard facts comprising educational content, and their optimal ordering for transmission to the student.[1]

Having survived that return to formalism, and the wild swing to the opposite extreme succeeding it in the late 1960s and early 1970s, we are now heading back in the old formalistic direction, with the insouciant amnesia that has become a hallmark of our educational history. Then, the slogans were "excellence," "mastery," "structure," and "discipline," and the devices were teaching machines, programmed instruction, and new school curricula prepared by experts in the disciplines. Now, the slogans are "excellence," "basics," "minimum competences," and "standards," and the devices are television and, more particularly, the computer. Then as now, the rhetoric was couched in broad educational terms, but economic incentives were also

Presented 18 April 1985 in the Schumann Distinguished Lecturer Series sponsored by the Interactive Technology in Education Program, at the Harvard Graduate School of Education, with the support of the Schumann Foundation. Reprinted from *Teachers College Record* 87, no. 4 (1986): 513–28.

at work, and educational motivations were powered by international rivalry. Sputnik was, to be sure, a Soviet achievement, whereas the feared plan for a fifth generation computer is Japanese. Are we, nevertheless, simply experiencing a déjà vu, watching a rerun where only the names have been changed to protect the innocent of history?

I think not. There are certainly salient parallels of the sort just outlined—parallels of ideological direction and emphasis, of terminology and motivation. But two differences stand out. First, the progressivism against which the earlier formalism reacted was milder than the antiestablishmentarianism of the 1960s and 1970s, and plumbed shallower emotional depths in the nation at large. The antiestablishment trend of the recent period, tied as it was to the upheaval over the Vietnam war, the youth movement, and efforts to improve the status of minorities, had wider ramifications in society at large; it went far beyond the schools. The social, political and educational reactions it has called forth have been correspondingly stronger and broader.

Second, the earlier formalism was independently narrower in its focus. It addressed the schools primarily, its vanguard composed of disciplinary scholars reforming school curricula, its technologies largely school-based. By contrast, the current technologies are broadly social in their impact; they are transforming society at large, and only secondarily the schools. Our children are living in a world already fundamentally altered by the television environment outside the school. They are growing into a world increasingly computerized in every sphere—industry, commerce, communications, transport, health care, science, government, and the military. Current technology is no mere affair of curriculum scholars. The school is now the tail, the whole world the computerized dog.

Indeed, the feeling that the computer revolution, since it is so pervasive, *must* be reflected in the school's basic offerings is widespread. Educators solemnly recommend computer literacy as a basic subject of study, advertisers frighten parents into buying computers so as to avert educational disaster for their children, salesmen present the computer as an instrument of achievement both in school and in life. In 1984, parents spent $110 million on educational software alone, it was reported by Future Computing, Inc., according to the *New York Times* of 11 November 1984.[2] Swept by computer frenzy, the community is urged to express it in home and in classroom no less than in other major institutions. If the general expansion of computerization is in fact here to stay, what are schools and educators to do? What *can* they do?

I suggest three things. First, they can take a critical attitude toward the pressures for computerization being brought to bear on education, recognizing that educational applications of the computer are not given or foreordained. There may indeed be good reasons of an educational sort for putting computers to use in the classroom. But I emphasize "of an educational sort."

Mere faddishness, or corporation hype, or status-seeking, or parental panic, or widespread social use are not enough. Second, taking an educational point of view regarding the computer, they can raise not only questions of effectiveness but also questions of value, alternatives, and side effects—ends as well as means. Third, they can be alert to the transfer of computer language to education and the consequent hazard that educational ends will be constricted to fit. In the remainder of my remarks, I shall elaborate on each of these three recommendations in turn.

These recommendations, it should be emphasized, are addressed primarily to educators rather than to the computer community. And I make bold to offer them despite my status as an outsider to this community because the use of the computer in education raises basic issues that are *general* rather than *technical,* and of serious concern to all of us.

I. The Illusion of Givenness

My recommendations, you will note, do not imply an antitechnology attitude. They do not urge educators to mount the barricades and fight the marauding technologists under the faded banner of humanism. There is, in fact, a know-nothingism about technology as there is a know-nothingism about pure science, arts, and humanities. Technology is no "evil empire" pitted in ultimate warfare against the realm of humane values. It is, after all, the transformation of the world through thought and, as such, essential and inescapable. Thought is ineffective without technique, technique impossible without thought. As John Passmore has put it: "Technology, the application of science, is itself an exercise of the human intelligence, the human imagination, the human gift for understanding. The pure mathematician who is reported to have rejoiced: 'Well, thank God, no one will ever find a use for *that* piece of mathematics' is as ridiculous a figure as the Philistine depicted by Matthew Arnold, with his monotonous refrain, "What's in it for me?' "[3] The invention and development of the computer, specifically, are triumphs of the creative mind that all can applaud.

Yet it does not follow that the computer must therefore be regarded as a given for education. The illusion of givenness is largely an offshoot of strong independent pressures for computerization. There is, in fact, no necessity that compels an advancing technology to be mirrored in school offerings, nothing fated about it. We do well to note that the Japanese themselves, our primary competitors in the computing field, have not rushed to install computers in the classroom, relying instead on their traditional culture of schooling coupled with intensive academic work and school-family supports.[4] And Professor Joseph Weizenbaum has reminded us of earlier technological enthusiasms, pointing to the example of home movie cameras gathering dust in thousands of closets across the nation, by contrast with the rosy promise of home computers humming in a swelling crescendo from coast to coast.[5]

I have described the illusion of givenness as largely an offshoot of the pressure for computerization. There is, I suggest, also a deeper source, that is, the absolutizing of the computer as a means. Let me explain. The computer as a symbol-manipulating device for accomplishing various purposes in industry, management, research, and so forth is not *ipso facto* a means for achieving educational purposes. Its instrumental value does not automatically carry over from the former to the latter. To suppose it does is to absolutize its status as a means.

The point deserves some elaboration. To speak of an object as an instrument is to convey some implicit reference to a purpose. In abstraction from purpose, no object is an instrument or, what comes to the same thing, there are no all-purpose means. To describe a hammer as a tool is to imagine some purpose to which it is to be put, some context in which such a purpose is embedded. The concept of a means is a relational rather than a categorical one.

It follows that instrumentality for a designated purpose implies nothing about instrumentality for any other. A hammer's usefulness for driving nails says nothing about its suitability as a soup ladle. Nor, on the other hand, does it follow that driving nails is the only purpose to which it can be put. The stereotype of an object may indeed tend to constrict our thought of it to its standard or conventional use, but the stereotype is itself no more intrinsic to the object than its instrumentality. If a hammer *cannot* serve as a soup ladle, it *can* serve as a doorstop, or a bookend, or a paper weight. Its suitability for such nonconventional uses is neither guaranteed nor precluded by its stereotype but must be independently established for each case.

What holds for the hammer holds for any technology. That an object is described as a technological device bears implicit reference to a purpose; its usefulness for such purpose in itself neither implies nor excludes its fitness for any other. The property of being a piece of technology is not a physical but a teleological property. It is not given but acquired with purpose.

To question the educational usefulness of the computer is thus no denial of its usefulness in all sorts of other ways. Nor does its undoubted value in other of its roles imply anything about its value for education. To put the computer to educational use is in fact to transform it from one sort of instrument to another, to change its character as technology by throwing it into a new combination with human purpose. Its instrumental value for education is not a foregone fact, "out there," decreed by history. *What* our purposes are, *which* of these we choose to implement, *how* we apply our resources to the effort—these make all the difference, and not merely to the application of technology but to its very constitution as such.

II. Educational Ends and Means

What educational purposes might then be served by computers? The answers that have been suggested are numerous, and they will no doubt continue to proliferate. I will comment on four of these, not by any means to provide definitive appraisals, but only to illustrate the sorts of questions that should, I believe, be addressed to such proposals.

1. One answer that has been given is that training in computers would provide marketable skills to children growing up in an increasingly computerized world. The computer's role is that of a vocational educator, preparing the masses of our youth for jobs in the future. This answer has been disputed. It has been argued that while some of our youth will obtain employment as computer experts, the promise of such employment to the general student body is empty. Professors Levin and Rumberger, for example, hold that "the proliferation of high technology industries and their products is far more likely to reduce the skill requirements of jobs in the U.S. economy than to upgrade them." And Professor Papert has been quoted as saying that because computer technology is advancing so rapidly, "what children are learning today [about computers] is going to be irrelevant when they get out of school."[6]

All our youth will of course be affected by the computer in a myriad of ways. They will become familiar with it and its effects in banks, schools, businesses, laboratories, supermarkets, hospitals, and libraries. But does it follow that, because these effects are widespread, the jobs will be as well? Should the masses of our youth be trained for Hollywood because of the prevalence of the movies, or for Detroit because of the widespread effects of the automobile? The question of future employment possibilities is, of course, an empirical one. There is, at any rate, no direct inference to be drawn from the social pervasiveness of the computer to the reliable promise of pervasive employment.

Even were such promise true, it would not follow that schools should provide the requisite training. Corporations and businesses have frequently argued, with respect to vocational education generally, that schools can best contribute to the general education of their students and to the development of students' social skills and character, leaving the rest to on-the-job experience. Whatever the truth may be on this issue, such alternatives must at least be explored. Again, it is worth noting the Japanese experience, in which schools have so far retained their traditional orientations, while the youth have acquired familiarity with the computer through informal means.

2. A second answer is more modest. It argues that schools should prepare students in a general way for the computerized world they will inhabit. This answer does not promise the youth employment in programming for they will, in all likelihood, be consumers of programs rather than producers. However, so the argument runs, any child not prepared to deal generally with computers in the future will be handicapped in a variety of ways— personal, social, and economic, no matter what occupation he or she may follow. For even as a consumer of programs, the child will require facility

with computers and at least some understanding of the process of programming. Some such line of thought seems to underlie the notion of "computer literacy," merging as well with the "minimum competency" rhetoric and the "basic skills" idea. The role of the computer is here envisaged not as a species of vocational education but as perhaps akin to driver education in supplying our youth with abilities without which they would be handicapped in life.

Now let us concede that a general knowledge of, and familiarity with, the computer will indeed be essential for adequate functioning in the future and, as such, desirable. Does it follow that *schools* should invest a significant effort in this direction? Exactly what type and what level of knowledge are, in fact, thought to be required? Do the requisite abilities presuppose a theoretical understanding of computer science or only one or another degree of operational facility? The way in which such questions are answered makes all the difference in the world in determining the school's proper role.

How many drivers understand the theory of the internal combustion engine? How many telephone or television users have analogous theoretical understanding? Driver education, premised on the public interest in traffic safety, leads no one to exalt "driver science" to the level of a New Basic Skill, along with English and mathematics, as the recent U.S. report *A Nation at Risk* does for computer science.[7] Yet if only operational facility is involved in either case, why the disparity? It might be suggested that the level of operational understanding required of the computer consumer is significantly higher than that required of the automobile consumer, but a detailed argument would have to be made to this effect. In any case, it would further need to be argued that the school is the preferred locus for acquiring such understanding, rather than out-of-school experience. It is ironic that academic formalists, providing neither argument, often advocate a computer literacy that may require no formal schooling at all, or at best at a level comparable to that of driver education.

3. A third answer is that the computer would enhance the learning of traditional school subjects. Unlike the previous two answers, which urged the importance of learning *about* the computer, the present answer advocates *using* the computer to learn about other things. The idea is to have the computer pick up the rote and repetitive aspects of traditional learning, providing as much individualized drill, practice, feedback, and evaluation as may be needed to reach suitable levels of mastery. The computer is here thought of as a mechanical drill sergeant or, more generally, as a mechanical teacher's aide.

As such, the computer has undoubted assets. It can connect with the student's learning process at any level and carry it further, in a manner unhampered by personal biases or social prejudices. It is also enormously patient (so to speak), providing as much practice and response as may be needed by the student to achieve any degree of mastery of school subjects.

Behind some of the recent talk of computer literacy lurks perhaps this idea as well: that facility with the computer will enable its use to drill students in the basic skills associated with academic subjects.

Whether such use would indeed be generally effective in developing skills and improving academic learning is an empirical question on which I am glad to defer to educational practitioners and researchers. I consider here only whether an affirmative answer would imply that schools should adopt such use forthwith.

Effectiveness would not in itself, I suggest, warrant such a conclusion. Any means effective in achieving a given end will have costs, side effects, further consequences, and alternatives, all of which require consideration. A recent *New York Times* article reports the insight that flashcards may rival the computer in teaching rote materials. "Children may initially be more willing to learn their multiplication tables with a computer-graphics program than with flashcards because of the novelty of the learning device. But the motivation often wears off quickly because the process of rote learning is no more creatively addressed on the screen than it is with cards."[8]

In general, one would at least need to consider such questions as the following before moving directly from computer effectiveness to school adoption: What alternative methods might be employed to the same end? What would be the relative social and economic costs? What would be the expected effects on equal access for all children? What consequences might be anticipated for school structure, student motivation, teacher training, school curricula, and the social and moral climate of learning? These questions are not meant to be rhetorical. I list them not as a way of rejecting the proposed use of the computer in the school, but only to argue that they require consideration. Such consideration might well sustain the proposal in question. But it would do so on grounds that go beyond the mere effectiveness of the computer in drilling students in basic skills.

One potential side effect is worth special mention. Effective use of the computer in the manner proposed here might encourage complacency with respect to basic skills; such complacency might, in turn, slight other uses of the computer for education in higher-level skills. A related effect seems already to have occurred in connection with the general recent emphasis on so called basics. The *New York Times* of 14 April 1983 thus describes educators as interpreting the recent mathematics survey of the National Assessment for Educational Progress as showing "an emerging trend in the nation's schools: younger students are improving in the basics and older students are doing worse in high-level skills." The report attributed "much of the positive change . . . to improved performance on rather routine items." However, "in general, students made much more modest gains, or no gains at all, on items assessing deep understanding or applications of mathematics."[9]

The president of the National Council of Teachers of Mathematics, Stephen S. Willoughby, was quoted by the *Times* as saying that "the only things we see improvement on—basic calculations—are things that a calculator can do better than a person. There is no way we can survive if kids do well only on trivial skills and don't show an understanding at a high level." In both reading and mathematics there seemed to be a similar pattern, according to Mary M. Lindquist, who is quoted in the same *Times* report: "In both subjects, we may be concentrating on those skills that are easiest to teach and learn and neglecting the thinking skills that are not so easily taught and learned."[10] The moral seems to be that while basic skills need to be learned, higher skills also require nurture. Putting the computer to work on effective drilling in the basics ought not to fill us with such educational self-righteousness that we forget about developing higher-level capacities.

4. This leads us to the fourth answer to our main question. This answer is that the computer should be used to help develop creative problem-solving abilities. Rather than serving primarily as an adjunct to the traditional academic subjects, the computer is to be used to promote logical, cognitive, and reasoning abilities—what may be called, speaking generally, critical thinking, inclusive of inventive approaches to problems. The computer is to be not a drill sergeant but rather a trainer or coach in developing the student's capacity to solve problems.

This proposal has several of the same advantages as those of the previous one. Its interaction with the student is free of biases, it can be prolonged to any degree necessary for the learning task in question, and it lends itself to individualization of instruction. The question of its effectiveness in promoting critical thinking is, as before, an empirical question. But the setting of suitable criteria of success is here more controversial than in the case of drilling for mastery of basic skills, and involves more urgently the question of transfer. And, assuming the method to be effective by any suitable criteria, questions analogous to those raised for the previous case would be relevant here as well, for example, questions of cost, alternatives, side effects, and further consequences.

On one issue, the present idea has an advantage over the last one. It places emphasis on higher-level, creative capacities, offering a maximal rather than a minimal vision of cognitive competences to be fostered. It tends in this way to counter the image of education as bounded by the familiar academic *subjects,* and to import the notion of *problems* as primary. Thus it moves to break out of the formalist mold that associates the computer with a hard education in the traditional subjects. But empirical evaluation remains to be dealt with, that is, are there determinate criteria of success by which the computer can be shown to offer advantages in promoting creative problem solving capacities?

An indefinite number of further applications of the computer to education might be devised. Nothing I have said implies that only the above four are possible or that they are the most desirable. I have used my four examples rather to illustrate the point that no computer use is inevitable and that every such use ought to run the gauntlet of questions ranging beyond considerations of effectiveness.

III. Computer Language

I want now to consider a large-scale side effect of computer use—the impact of computer language on our conception of educational ends. Specifically, I address the potential constriction of such ends through our hypnotic fascination with the computer.

The question to be raised here is not one of efficiency in achieving the ends designated; I concede, for the sake of the present argument, that the computer has been empirically shown to be effective in any or all of the ways previously discussed. It is precisely when our means are effective in achieving certain ends that we are tempted to lose sight of other and more elusive ends.

I have already mentioned the emphasis on basic skills as having encouraged the neglect of higher-level capacities. Similarly, "teaching to the test" is easier than teaching for understanding; teaching facts and habits is easier than teaching methods and dispositions. I spoke earlier of the *absolutizing of means*. What concerns me now is the *expansion of means* at the expense of ends.

Nor is this tendency peculiar to education. We naturally tend to shrink our vision of the world to our mode of access to it. As infants, we have to learn that there are objects beyond our field of vision; as we grow, we must continually expand our imaginative construction of the world beyond experience. Throughout life, our perception favors those things assimilable to our categories, rubrics, and models; what does not fit is noted only with difficulty. As researchers, we tend to identify our problems with those questions answerable by our chosen methods. It is no wonder that the phenomenon repeats itself again and again in the field of education.

The general point is this: as the computer's presence grows, the whole array of our educational ends tends to shrink to what is achievable or supposedly achievable by computer. Instead of understanding the computer as a means to goals independently sought, we tend to redefine our goals so as to match what computers may do. From its initial status as a technology for promoting independently specified educational values, the computer thus becomes transformed into a general criterion of value. And the whole process is facilitated by language transfer.

Even without hard evidence for the educational efficacy of the computer, the mere promise of such efficacy promotes the transfer of computer language to education. Such transfer tends to filter out ends and values that do not fit the metaphor—for example, ethical sensitivity, social perceptiveness, artistic

expressiveness—so that the efficiency of the computer is expanded by definition. For it is the merest tautology that ends achievable by the computer are
achievable by the computer. It is, however, far from tautological that all
educational ends are indeed achievable by the computer. Indeed, it is false,
and it impoverishes education in fundamental ways.

There is a certain irony in this development. While computer language
has promoted a reductive view of the realm of teleological and mental
process, teleological language has enriched the view of computer processes.
Thus, computer scientists and cyberneticists have increasingly employed
teleological and, indeed, anthropomorphic language in working with the
computer. They have also tried to simulate certain mental processes with
their admittedly partial models, then transferring the unreduced teleological
descriptions of such processes to these models. At the same time, researchers
and educators have increasingly applied computer terminology to the mind
and have tried to reduce mental functions to those of the machine, the whole
reductive effort threatening to run in a logical circle.[11] How far we now are
from a *genuine* reduction of mind may be illustrated by a recent comment
of Professor Shimon Ullman, head of the Weizmann Institute's National
Center for Artificial Intelligence (AI). According to Ullman:

> The main message of *AI* research seems to be that those areas once consid-
> ered inordinately difficult—such as designing a computer that can play
> world class chess—have proven relatively simple, whereas teaching a com-
> puter elementary tasks, such as understanding English or visually discern-
> ing shapes, [has] proved nearly impossible. The main objective is to learn
> more about the brain through this research. The reason we're not sure just
> how to make computers intelligent is that we still aren't certain what goes
> on in the brain.[12]

Looked at from the point of view of research, the transfer of languages
from one realm to another exemplifies a creative strategy, often leading to
progress. Certain analogies are suggestive enough to justify such transfers in
the present case even if computers do not literally think and the mind is not
literally a computer. One needs only to avoid making circular reductive
claims. But looked at from the point of view of educational practice, the
matter is more serious. For the computer-metaphor acts to screen out what
may be of the first importance, educationally speaking. The challenge confronting educators is to adopt whatever advantages computer uses may be
shown to offer, while holding fast to their independent vision of educational
values.

The computer-metaphor, as I intend this phrase, is not a single metaphor,
but actually a cluster of several related metaphors, operating in different
ways and at different levels. Nor—and I emphasize this—is the computer-

metaphor bound to the strict understanding of the computer by the experts. It generates its force also, or even largely, from public conceptions of the matter, whether accurate or not. I want, in what follows, to concentrate on one major metaphor belonging to the cluster, that centered on the notion of *information*.

IV. The Notion of Information

A prevalent public image of the computer is, surely, that of an information processor. Information comes in discrete bits, each expressing a factual datum. Data may be entered and stored in the computer's memory, retrieved from memory, and processed in simple or complex ways according to various programs, which instruct the computer exactly what functions to perform. These functions are in the nature of algorithms, specifying determinately how the data are to be transformed. The human operator determines that the solution to his problem might be computed by program from input data, punches in his instructions to the machine to institute the relevant program, and eventually sees the solution displayed on the screen before him.

Now, to think of learning, generally, in these terms is undeniably suggestive. But see how much is left out of the picture. Learning takes place not just by computing solutions to problems, nor even just by exchanging words, but by emulation, observation, identification, wonder, supposition, dream, imitation, doubt, action, conflict, ambition, participation, and regret. It is a matter of insight and perception, invention and self-knowledge, intimation and feeling, as much as of question and answer. Even the understanding of an answer in everyday life involves catching not just the information literally conveyed by the words, but also what is expressed by their overtones and nuances and what is carried between the lines or in the silences. Such understanding is not, in general, reducible to computation.

The activity of the computer operator, in the public's mind, is isolated and cognitive, its vehicles the finger and the eye. But even our cognitive skills are social. They grow in the first instance out of interactions with others more skilled than we, in continuous processes of discussion, demonstration, and exchange. The activity of a learner involves all of his being. It is moral and muscular, visceral and vascular, social and historical, proceeding, in Dewey's words, by trying and by undergoing.

Learning advances not only when new answers are gained but also when old answers are lost, not only when problems are solved but also when solutions turn problematic. Indeed, the categories of question-answering and problem-solving are too meager to contain such educational successes as new competences formed, new attitudes crystallized, new loyalties shaped, new discriminations made, new appraisals formulated, new emotions felt, new insights gained, new challenges undertaken, new purposes assumed.

Interactive technology is but the tiniest sliver of interactive life. Unless, indeed, one had been learning all one's life and in multifarious ways before one's first approach to a computer, one could hardly learn anything *from* the machine. What questions could one put, what purposes could one have, what significance could one possibly attach to the answers received?

The computer-metaphor, as just considered, projects the situation of the computer operator onto the learner generally. Now consider another, and deeper, application of the metaphor, in which the learner is seen not as the operator but as the computer itself. Like the computer, the learner acquires information, stores it in memory, ready to retrieve and process it in order to solve the problems put to him or her. But here is the catch: the computer does not pose its own problems to itself, but requires an operator to do so, an operator with needs and purposes of his own. Without such needs and purposes, what constitutes a problem? What data require retrieval, and to what end? What functions ought to be activated, what needs fulfilled, what lacks satisfied? What can be the significance of information without appraisal in light of aims? Knowledge of one's enduring aims and purposes is, furthermore, not just another body of information, but a form of insight into the patterning of one's chosen problems, the setting of one's life tasks.

To speak of information and memory, not to mention knowledge, in reference to the computer, is itself a metaphorical transfer from the human case. To transfer such terms back from the computer to the mind, now emptied of the connotations of human activity, interpretation, need, and purpose, is an example of the irony I mentioned earlier. This double transfer in the context of practice leads us unwittingly to shrink our initial ideals of education and our conceptions of mind and schooling.

The everyday notion of information refers to material we can understand and interpret in context. Grasping what it expresses, we can paraphrase it and evaluate its contextual relevance, criticize and reject it or back it up appropriately, respond to it with feeling, sense its metaphorical echoes, appraise its bearing on our purposes, and apply it in our activity. The computer itself cannot be properly described as doing any of these things, in the everyday senses of the terms involved. To characterize the electronic state of computer circuitry in terms of "information" is to employ the word under a different interpretation. Further to construe the mind in terms of "computer information" empties the human notion of virtually all its content.

It is important to emphasize that even in its full-blooded human sense, the concept of information is far from capable of adequately expressing our educational aims. This is so even if we concentrate on the purely cognitive aims of schooling, as they relate to the enterprise of problem-solving. For although information is certainly essential to education, it is only part of the story. Consider: you can be given a piece of information but fail to realize its significance either for the problem at hand or for action, more generally. You can accept that such and such is the case but be totally unable to give any good reasons for it, thus disqualifying yourself as really knowing that such and such is the case. You can know it but not recall it at the fitting moment, or recall it but be unable to apply it intelligently to the problem under consideration. You may indeed be *able* to apply it without being in general *disposed* to do so, not having formed the suitable inclination or character trait. The suggestion that at least the cognitive side of education can be fully expressed in terms of information transfer, storage, and retrieval would not be worth a moment's consideration were it not that it is implicitly conveyed by the current formalism, coupled with the public's awe of scientific facts.

To know a fact requires, however, as Gilbert Ryle has put it, "having taken it in, i.e., being able and ready to operate with it, from it, around it and upon it. To possess a piece of information is to be able to mobilize it apart from its rote-neighbors and out of its rote-formulation in unhackneyed and *ad hoc* tasks."[13] Now the Baconian image of science as an increasing accumulation of facts has independently distorted the ideal of education since well before the computer age. With "facts" now translated into "bits of information," the Baconian image is given modern dress. Just see how contemporary Mr. Gradgrind sounds when his little speech in Dickens's *Hard Times* is altered by replacing the word "fact" with "information." He is explaining his educational views to a teacher in the school he manages. I reproduce here the original passage, but you can mentally make the replacement at each occurrence of the word "Fact" or "Facts":

> "Now what I want is Fact. Teach these boys and girls nothing but Facts. Facts alone are wanted in life. Plant nothing else, root out everything else. You can form the mind of reasoning animals upon Facts; nothing else will be of any service to them."[14]

The teacher addressed by Mr. Gradgrind agrees. He has learned and proposes to teach his students "about all the Water Sheds of all the world and all the histories of all the peoples, and all the names of all the rivers and mountains, and all the productions, manners and customs of all the countries, and all their boundaries and bearings on the two and thirty points of the compass."[15]

Mr. Gradgrind considered the learning of such facts to be hard work. Current formalists think it can be made fun. The educational game selected as the best of 1984 by *Electronic Games* magazine, according to the *New York Times,* is one in which the player "must destroy the Fuzzbomb before it spreads across the entire nation. To confront the Fuzzbomb, the player or agent takes trains from city to city to get to the Fuzzbomb's location, which continually changes."[16] The presumed charm of this game is supposed to facilitate the student's learning to identify the state capitals. The same principle could no doubt be applied to the Water Sheds of all the world, and other such important facts.

Facts are, however, not the sorts of things imagined by Gradgrinds past or present. They are expressed in language, clothed in concepts, organized and transformed by theory, appraised by criteria of value, and intelligently or stupidly employed in the conduct of life. Neither the concepts nor the values we possess are automatically derivable from hard facts or data; they serve rather to mold the forms in which our putative facts are cast. These facts provide tests of our theories through their own credibilities, but they do not generate these theories by any kind of routine processing. They are, in turn, responsive to our theories and tested by them. That we have the theories and facts we do is therefore a reflection not only of our mental capacities or of the "real world," but of our history and our intellectual heritage.

Even the capacity for *intelligent use* of information will not suffice to express our educational aims relative to problem-solving. Drawing on accumulated data is inadequate for accommodation to future change. What is wanted in addition is the generation of new information—information, moreover, that does not result simply from applying old categories to new circumstances. Devising new categories, composing new classifications, postulating new entities, guessing at new connections, inventing new languages and calculi are desiderata of the highest importance.

Problem-solving, further, needs not just the recognition and retention of facts but the recognition and retention of difficulties, incongruities, and anomalies. It does not simply affirm truths but entertains suppositions, rejects the accepted, conceives the possible, elaborates the doubtful or false, questions the familiar, guesses at the imaginable, improvises the unheard-of. An intelligence capable only of storing and applying truths would be profoundly incapacitated for the solving of problems.

When we move beyond problem-solving to consider educational aims in general, we find the computer-metaphor based on "information" to be even more clearly inadequate. For we here encounter provinces long cultivated by rival metaphors, alien to the impression or transmission of facts. What I have elsewhere called the *insight model*[17] is one such rival metaphor. It speaks not of information but of insight and perception, vision and illumination, intuition of nuance and pattern, grasp of overtone and undertone.

A second such rival metaphor is that of *equipping*,[18] or the provision of skills and capacities. This is not a matter of storing answers, whether linguistic or numerical, and it cannot be accommodated solely in information-theoretic terms. It concerns rather the forming or strengthening of abilities, the know-*how* commanded by a person, rather than the know-*that*, the capability to deal with the tasks and challenges of practice in the various domains of life. Nor is every bit of *know-how* accessible to algorithm— witness the comic's ability to make us laugh, the actor's capacity to make us weep, and the metaphorical ability itself, beyond the regimented interpretation of literal codes.

A third such rival metaphor is represented by what I have called the *rule model*.[19] This metaphor focuses on norms rather than capacities, on the proneesses, likelihoods, tendencies, and dispositions of a person rather than on his mere abilities and skills—on what he *does* do rather than what he *can* do. In this realm we have again left the notion of information behind. For what is involved here is not the storing or transformation of data, but the shaping of habits of mind and feeling, the growth of attitudes and traits, the development of character. Our concern is not with knowing *that* nor even with knowing *how*. For we are dealing not with what people believe, nor with what they are equipped to do, but with what they can reliably be expected to do, with their predictable but typically unarticulated patterns of conduct, taste, and emotion. The inculcation of desirable patterns of this sort, beyond the reach of algorithms, is of the first educational importance, laying the foundations of mutual trust, common feeling, and shared value without which no community can stand, let alone thrive.

These various realms all require to be kept steadfastly in view as we make progress on any educational front. The whole array of ends must serve as the context within which we gauge our educational situation. Rather than cutting this array down to the size of our technology, we should strive to look beyond our technology, to determine the purposes and directions of our further efforts.

The computer has been associated with the recent swing to hard education, with the notion of raising standards, of higher achievement in academic subjects, of increased efficiency in the teaching of fact, of enhanced problem-solving capacity. All these matters are indeed important. There is no positive virtue in low academic achievement, inefficient teaching, or diminished problem-solving capacity. Whatever the computer may be able to accomplish in such areas is all to the good. No such accomplishment, however, should block our vision of equally vital educational goals, or shrink our highest ideals of learning. It is the task of educators to keep both means and ends in view.[20]

Notes

1. I. Scheffler, "Concepts of Education: Reflections on the Current Scene," in *Guidance in American Education: Backgrounds and Prospects,* ed. Edward Landy and Paul. A. Perry (Cambridge, Mass.: Harvard Graduate School of Education, distributed by Harvard University Press, 1964); reprinted in Israel Scheffler, *Reason and Teaching* (London: Routledge & Kegan Paul, 1973), p. 59.

2. Peggy Schmidt, "What to Look for in Educational Software," *The New York Times,* Section 12 (Education, Fall Survey), 11 November 1984, p. 8.

3. John Passmore, *The Philosophy of Teaching* (Cambridge, Mass.: Harvard University Press, 1980), p. 115.

4. See Merry I. White, "Japanese Education: How Do They Do It?" *The Public Interest* 76 (1984): 87–101. White writes: "Computers and other technology do not play a large role in (Japanese) schools. . . . There is no national program to develop high technology skills in children. Americans spend much more money on science and technology in the schools; the Japanese spend more on teacher training and salaries" (p. 90).

5. In an address to the Philosophy of Education Research Center, Harvard University, Fall 1983. I am grateful to Professor Weizenbaum, whose pioneering critical reflections on the computer have taught me much. See especially his book *Computer Power and Human Reason* (San Francisco, Calif.: W. H. Freeman, 1976).

6. See Henry M. Levin and R. W. Rumberger, "The Educational Implications of High Technology," Project Report No. 83-A4, Institute for Research on Educational Finance and Governance, Stanford University, February 1983. These authors argue that "the expansion of the lowest skilled jobs in the American economy will vastly outstrip the growth of high technology ones" (abstract, ibid.).

   See also *The Boston Globe,* 26 November 1984, p. 42, which also quotes Seymour Papert as calling "absurd" the "fear that children will be unprepared for the job market they face on graduation unless they have become 'computer literate.' "

7. National Commission on Excellence in Education, *A Nation at Risk,* U.S. Department of Education, Washington, D.C.: Government Printing Office, 26 April 1983.

8. Schmidt, "What to Look for in Educational Software."

9. *The New York Times,* 14 April 1983.

10. Ibid.

11. Cf. the pioneering paper of Arturo Rosenblueth, Norbert Wiener, and Julian Bigelow, "Behavior, Purpose, and Teleology," *Philosophy of Science* 10 (1943): 18–24, which argues that the concept of "purposefulness" is "necessary for the understanding of certain modes of behavior" and that its importance has been slighted owing to the rejection of final causes as explanatory; the authors then go on to interpret purpose in terms of negative feedback.

   In my paper "Thoughts on Teleology," *British Journal for the Philosophy of Science* 9 (1959), and then in my book, *The Anatomy of Inquiry* (New York: Alfred A. Knopf, 1963; now Hackett, 1981), I argued that if the Rosenblueth, Wiener, and Bigelow paper simply extends teleological language to selected forms of behavior of independent interest, there can be no quarrel with them, "for in such a case, they would not be setting forth an analysis of teleology so much as striving to improve the description of the behavior in question through increased use of teleological language. If, however, as appears to be the case, they intend also to provide an *analysis* of teleological notions, their proposal may properly be judged by seeing how satisfactorily the analysis accounts for acknowledged instances of teleological behavior" (ibid., 112).

   My argument was that the authors' reduction of teleology to negative feedback does not succeed. But they thought it did and so, by their lights, weren't arguing in a circle. But, on my view, the claim to reduce human purpose to machine purpose by their method can achieve plausibility only by so enriching the latter as to encompass the former. But the trends I discuss in the text are quite general and go far beyond the above illustrative reference.

12. See *The Forward,* 8 March 1985, p. 33.

13. Gilbert Ryle, "Teaching and Training," in *The Concept of Education,* ed. R. S. Peters (London: Routledge & Kegan Paul, 1967), p. 111.

14. Charles Dickens, *Hard Times* (1854), chap. 1.

15. Ibid., chap. 2. p. 7.

16. Schmidt, "What to Look for in Educational Software."

17. Scheffler, *Reason and Teaching,* pp. 71ff.

18. Cf. Gilbert Ryle, *The Concept of Mind* (London: Hutchinson, 1949), p. 310: "In a word, teaching is deliberate equipping."

19. Scheffler, *Reason and Teaching,* pp. 76ff.

20. I should like to call attention to the summer 1984 issue of *Teachers College Record* 85, no. 4, which is devoted to discussions of the computer and education. Professor Douglas Sloan's editorial introduction to the issue carries the admirable title, "On Raising Critical Questions about the Computer in Education," ibid., p. 539.

    I also wish to call attention to Catherine Z. Elgin's critique of computer models of the mind, in her "Representation, Comprehension, and Competence," *Social Research* 51, no. 4 (Winter 1984): 906–25.

    Lastly, I am very grateful to my colleagues in the Philosophy of Education Research Seminar at Harvard, Catherine Elgin, Kenneth Hawes, Vernon Howard, David Perkins, and Paul Smeyers, for critical discussion of a draft of this article.

9

Moral Education beyond
Moral Reasoning

I.

Lawrence Kohlberg's important work[1] has been enormously influential within psychology. What is more surprising is its effect on philosophy, where it has evoked numerous responses from philosophers of various schools, both here and abroad. It matters not that many, perhaps most, of these responses have been to a greater or lesser degree critical. The interesting fact is that he managed to stimulate a new level of exchange between the two fields. I count this as one of Kohlberg's most important achievements.

How did he accomplish it? I suggest that three elements of his work were mainly responsible. First, he addressed himself systematically to a central area of life and thought—moral development. Second, he proposed serious and ambitious theses concerning such development. Finally, he acknowledged humanistic as well as scientific aspects of the subject, overriding conventional boundaries between the empirical and the philosophical, the descriptive and the normative, the factual and the conceptual.

Philosophers were at once captivated by Kohlberg's boldness, challenged by his grand and simple vision, and charmed by his friendly willingness to engage in cross-disciplinary debate. Somewhat weary of the prevalent microscopic style of philosophizing, they were delighted to find a psychologist propounding large doctrines affecting their own subject and claiming for such doctrines the authority of empirical inquiry. Cloistered meta-ethicists warily left their studies to scout the prospects of a collaborative effort by scientists and humanists to understand the nature of morality. Whatever the ultimate success of such effort, Kohlberg promoted it as an ideal worthy of pursuit in an increasingly distracted and fragmented world, badly in need both of morality and collaboration.

Paper presented at a memorial meeting for Lawrence Kohlberg, Harvard University, 1988. Published in Dawn Schroder, ed., "The Legacy of Lawrence Kohlberg," in *New Directions for Child Development*, no. 47 (San Francisco, Jossey-Bass, 1990), pp. 99–102.

II.

Both the substance of Kohlberg's system and the responses to it have, however, grown more elaborate over the years. So much ink has by now been spilled in discussion of the fine points of this or that version that it would be profitless for me to add to such discussion here. The nature and reality of his postulated moral stages, their presumed necessary and invariant order, the evidence for such order, the technique of his interviews, the rationale of his scoring method—all have generated mountains of controversy and commentary, not to mention internal alterations in response, so that the system has presented a continually "moving target" for skeptics and critics. Indeed, the methodological questions in particular have by now grown so complex that philosophers who initially came relishing a broad and simple vision of the subject now confront a prospect no less microscopic than their own.

I therefore gladly leave such questions of detail to my psychologist colleagues and address myself here to a broader question: What is the import of Kohlberg's work for moral education and what are its limitations? First, as to its import, he stresses the importance of moral reasoning, the background principles and considerations that guide our moral judgments. In Socratic spirit, he emphasizes the role of knowledge of the good in the moral life; in Kantian spirit, he values consistency, universality, autonomy, and respect for persons.

These are certainly fundamental aspects of morality in my view, and they fully deserve the critical role assigned to them in Kohlberg's scheme. The recent suggestion that an ethic of care is to be counterposed as an alternative to an ethic of principles has never seemed to me persuasive since respect for persons is a high, perhaps the highest, form of care—while care in any case requires to be apportioned equitably. It is worth recalling that Kant himself deduces the duty of helping those in need from his universalization principle; to promote a generally uncaring world, free of "love and sympathy," as he describes it, is, for him, a contradiction in the will.[2]

Nevertheless, crucial as is proper reasoning to the moral life, and therefore to moral education, it has its natural limits. Nothing can indeed substitute for such reasoning, yet reasoning cannot stand alone. A full moral education requires other things *in addition to* appropriate reasoning, even if there is no question of such things *replacing* it. Moral education is thus, I believe, irreducible to moral development, under the particular construction given such development in Kohlberg's work.

I make this point not in criticism of his work as such—Kohlberg might conceivably have agreed with the thrust of my remarks—but rather to counteract the temptation to suppose that his work offers a complete account of moral education and a total guide to its practice. For this supposition of completeness—which is in fact no part of Kohlberg's doctrine itself—has unfortunately captured the public imagination, ever in search of educational panaceas.

What else, then, is required for moral education beyond proper moral reasoning? First, the establishment of basic forms of conduct; the foundations of character in action. Whatever their rationale, fundamental lines of decent behavior need to be laid down in practice and made second nature. The most sophisticated display of reasons will not redeem action that is habitually violent, deceptive, cruel, or contemptuous of others.

This Aristotelian point, in contrast to Kohlberg's Socratic view, is countered by his criticism of the so-called "bag of virtues approach," which, he argues, is unclear because it is irremediably context-bound. But vices are, I suggest, much clearer than virtues, and minimally decent conduct—which avoids such vices as injury to others as well as self-harm—can and should be expected as a fundamental stratum of moral education. I want desperately to walk through the streets free of bodily assault and am comparatively less concerned with the moral stage of my law-abiding fellow citizens. Conversely, I am not much consoled if, having been stabbed, I am informed that my attacker is moving up the ladder of moral development.

More generally, conformity to basic social rules sanctioned by context is prerequisite to taking hold of and modifying such rules later on. As in science and the arts, so in morality, acquisition of the inherited corpus is a base for further sophistication. Neither science nor art nor morality springs full-blown from the human mind. Without preliminary immersion in a tradition of practice—an appreciation of the force of its rules, obligations, rights, and demands—the concept of choice of actions and rules for oneself can hardly be achieved.

A second and related point bears not so much on Kohlberg's theory as on his method, which makes crucial use of the notion of dilemmas. Such use is theoretically benign, the intent being to elicit differences in the form of moral reasoning by application to hard cases. But the pernicious suggestion conveyed by such use is that moral behavior consists solely or primarily of hard cases—brain teasers and conundrums to which there are no decisive answers, a suggestion that reinforces the very relativism that Kohlberg sought to combat. As in the law, hard cases in morality must be conceived as presupposing a preponderance of easy cases, contingencies where decision poses no deep theoretical problems and where proper behavior may be appropriately expected to be second nature. Here again, an Aristotelian emphasis is important.

The two points I have made so far might be roughly described as having to do with moral content as opposed to the form of moral conduct. My last point concerns rather factual or historical content. If the whole of moral education consisted in the attainment of some presumed highest stage of moral reasoning, culture and history should make no difference: Socrates and Kant should be equally well-equipped morally no matter when or where they lived. But imagine them transplanted to twentieth-century Boston. They would be totally bewildered, not merely cognitively or factually, but morally. They would, I suggest, be not merely cognitively defective but morally defective—morally handicapped in the extreme—being unaware of the very nature of the acts and alternatives that present themselves daily to the contemporary agent in our society, and so unable fully to *apply* their principles to the great problems now confronting humanity. What could they possibly make of our commercial, industrial, or communications systems, of international finance, of multinational corporations, of international, political or military rivalry, of guerrilla warfare, of our ecological problems? The conclusion I find inescapable is that moral education cannot be skimmed off the top of history, or abstracted from its detail. You cannot be at once moral and ignorant. Facts have moral import.

Notes

1. Lawrence Kohlberg, *Essays on Moral Development,* vol. 1 (The Philosophy of Moral Development), San Francisco, Harper & Row 1981, and vol. 2 (The Psychology of Moral Development) San Francisco, Harper & Row, 1984.
2. Immanuel Kant, *Groundwork of the Metaphysic of Morals,* Chapter 2.

Part IV

Education

10

The Education of
Policy-Makers

How, ideally, ought the policy-maker to be educated? How, in particular, might a curriculum for educational decision-makers be conceived? The following attempt to answer these questions offers not a detailed blueprint but a set of basic guidelines, of central conceptions and attitudes that should, in my view, permeate a curriculum for makers of policy. Nor is this attempt concerned with formal courses of study to prepare policy-makers. The curriculum metaphor extends more widely to processes of learning that should go on throughout educational policy formulation, execution, and evaluation. And the metaphor applies, further, not just to the individual policy-maker but to all those whose attitudes and ideas affect the making of policy. To think of curriculum is useful if it helps us to answer the general question: What basic conceptions ought to inform the policy process?

Beyond Technique

There are important aspects of policy-making and evaluation that are technical in a relatively straightforward sense: they involve special knowledge or methods of analysis developed within a discipline or professional tradition. Questions relating, for example, to nutrition, neurological disability, statistical analysis, or agricultural procedures may all be considered technical in this sense. The layperson concerned with such questions is well advised to consider the results of the relevant special disciplines, or the consensus of their practitioners on these matters; such an individual cannot pronounce on these questions with any degree of confidence. If the layperson, moreover, aspires to a policy-making role, he or she must acquire at least a modicum of the relevant technical knowledge and a certain proficiency in

This paper is drawn from Chapter 4 of my *Of Human Potential: An Essay in the Philosophy of Education* (London: Routledge, 1985). It is reprinted from *Harvard Educational Review* 54, no. 2 (1984): 152–65.

forms of technical analysis and technical evaluation. But the policy-making role cannot be reduced wholly to technical matters.

First, in order for technical items, such as mathematical formulas, theoretical constructs, and special notations, to be properly understood and applied, their logical bases and methodological backgrounds have to be comprehended. What functions do such items serve in the larger context of inquiry? What are their conceptual structures and their empirical credentials? What alternatives, if any, are available within their respective disciplines? What limits on their interpretation are presupposed? Intelligent use of the results of a specialized inquiry requires a grasp of its underlying logic.

Second, each item of special knowledge must, in policy applications, be brought into contact with items drawn from other special studies. The integration of practical considerations stemming from different disciplines of research typically falls outside each discipline. The architect, for example, must thus deal with and relate the economic, physical, and sociological bearings of his or her design. Such integration is not given within any single discipline; it is not itself a further disciplinary specialty but rather a matter of professional art. It requires, first of all, a sensitivity to the languages and procedures of diverse special inquiries and an ability to link them, where possible, through translation, or partial translation. Beyond the reach of translation altogether, such integration requires that one accommodate the various items to one another in assigning them relevantly to different segments of the common problems.[1]

Reference to such common problems provides yet a third respect in which the policy role shows itself to be irreducible to the merely technical. For such problems arise not in a segregated domain ordered for the purposes of inquiry by a given discipline, but rather in the fullness of everyday life, the scene of multiple human activities, experiences, purposes, and needs. The awareness of such problems is not the monopoly of any special discipline, nor is it the exclusive province of any set of disciplines. Pooling the specialized perspectives of the several forms of inquiry does not yet guarantee human understanding. Such understanding, since it is addressed to the activities and feelings of people, requires access to the way those people understand themselves; it requires that we hear what they say when they speak in their own voice.[2]

The policy role, finally, requires self-consciousness respecting values. This is, of course, not meant to deny that the special disciplines are themselves guided by values; nor is it intended to resuscitate a general dichotomy of facts and values. The point is rather that the values of inquiry are in themselves insufficient to orient the response of professions to the diverse realms of practical life. To heal the sick is more than just to inquire into the healing of the sick, and it demands organization by its own appropriate principles of action.

I have listed four respects in which the policy role goes beyond the domain of technical knowledge and enters upon the humanistic realm. To gather these four aspects together and make them explicit as guidelines for the education of policy-makers is to conceive of the policy role in a distinctive way. This distinctiveness is best understood by seeing what it excludes. It excludes, first of all, the notion that results of special inquiries are hard-and-fast truths, to be accepted without question and applied directly to problems in whatever ways may seem plausible. The present conception, by contrast, insists that the scope and meaning of every result is qualified by its logical and methodological context. The policy-maker certainly need not, and cannot, become a specialist in every discipline relevant to his or her work, but should be able to raise critical questions addressed to the specialists, concerning their basic concepts and the basic logic of their argumentation.

Second, this conception excludes the notion that policy is the appendage of any single discipline. No discipline enjoys a unique purchase on the problems to be addressed. The education of a policy-maker, therefore, cannot be construed as a process merely of absorbing the abstractions of a single discipline, learning to speak its language and to map its hypotheses onto practice. The policy-maker needs to be multilingual, to learn to speak and hear various disciplinary dialects, and to employ them conjointly in understanding the problems.[3]

Third, this conception excludes the notion that the disciplines, taken singly or together, constitute the full conceptual equipment for policy roles. The policy-maker, under this conception, should be multilingual not only with respect to the several disciplines of inquiry, but also with respect to the ordinary languages of those people whose problems such inquiry addresses. For the very relevance of disciplinary findings is intrinsically qualified by the meanings such people may place on them.

Finally, this conception excludes the idea that the policy-maker is above or beyond the reach of value considerations, that his or her role is merely to pursue with maximal efficiency goals independently determined.[4] This conception, on the contrary, emphasizes the fusion of technical and value components of action; efficiency in intentional activity is a virtue if, and only if, the intention is proper. The agent of policy inescapably confronts both the question of value and the question of efficiency, if the agent is at all reflective. The policy-maker stands not outside the realm of value but squarely within it.

Policy and People

The human studies are reflexive in nature. Students of human culture and history are learning about themselves as well as about others. Their very efforts to give systematic accounts of human activity are comprehended by the accounts they give. As creatures of intention and action, they pursue their special goal of understanding intention and action by studying the self-conceptions of creatures like themselves.

Understanding their own actions in terms of their purposes and beliefs, their norms and the ideals they set for themselves, they seek a parallel understanding of others. That is to say, they strive to place the action of others within the framework of others' purposes and beliefs, norms, and ideals. The application of such a teleological explanation schema is of continuing importance in history, social science, psychology, literature, and everyday life.[5]

People taken as *objects of study* by social scientist and policy-maker alike are not for that reason to be thought of as *objects*. Insofar as the belief-purpose schema is thought relevant to an understanding of their actions, they are accorded a fundamental distinction from mere objects—things that may be symbolized but do not themselves symbolize; things that may be used to further various ends but that themselves form no ends.

Policy-makers concerned to understand people, as indeed they must, need to view them as subjects—active beings whose field of endeavor is structured by their own symbolic systems, their conceptions of world, self, and community, their memories of the past, perceptions of the present, and hopes for the future. Treating people as carbon copies of oneself, without taking the trouble to enter into their cultural environment, or—worse still—treating them as mere instrumentalities for, or hindrances to, the realization of a preconceived plan, is a formula for policy failure.

There is a second respect in which people are to be viewed as subjects. They are to be seen not simply as comprising a field of application for policy, but as a resource for its origination and evaluation. This attitude takes their reactions not merely as promising facilitation or defeat of policy but as offering occasions for the review of policy. The policy-maker's advance rationale is not sealed off from scrutiny *by* those, and communication *with* those, for whom policy is intended. His or her initial intentions are vulnerable to change, in principle, through interaction with the intentions of others.

Taking people as subjects means, then, *acknowledging* the existence of their perspectives and perceptions, and it means also *respecting* such perspectives in the formulation of one's own policies, giving no privileged role to one's own perspectives simply because they are one's own. The combination of acknowledgment of, and respect for, the equal powers of others to legislate rules for themselves is, as Kant taught, a recognition of human dignity. Such recognition means that human development cannot be construed as a shaping, by one agent, of another's life. The other's life is not a piece of clay to be shaped by the developer or the developer's policy. It has its own integrity, its own structure and movement. Any policy for development must take such reciprocity into account, and must therefore not pretend that its own goals are beyond question, its own vision of welfare decisive.

Recognition of human dignity as an ideal of policy is a matter of prizing peoples' powers to order their own lives; it is equally a matter of prizing social arrangements that honor such powers. Policy inescapably influences lives, but such influence is properly directed toward the enhancement of human dignity, thus interpreted: the aim of development is self-development. Equally, it is social development of a special sort—the growth of arrangements under which free human beings may regard one another with mutual respect for their shared intelligence and powers of choice.

Policy and Reflexivity

I have noted the reflexivity of the human studies, urging that in such studies the inquirer belongs implicitly to the subject matter itself. The effect of this point, made explicit, is to turn attention inward, to focus the policy-maker's awareness on the contribution he himself makes to the phenomena he addresses. The movement encouraged is the movement from a naively realist attitude to a self-conscious or critical attitude. Such an attitude is of major importance for the policy role as here conceived.

This attitude is, however, not a natural one; it requires special cultivation. Indeed, the heavy onus of policy responsibility in education militates strongly against it. Self-consciousness increases the burden of choice and enlarges the perception of uncertainty. The pervasive drive to simplify, to objectify, and to reduce is thus fully understandable. Educational potentials, for example, have accordingly been petrified into fixed attributes of the child's nature, uniformly positive in value and, as a set, harmoniously realizable. Multiple problems of choice have been reduced to the problem of realizing most efficiently those potentials now manifest. The policy-maker's attention has been focused outward, on the child and on technique. The present treatment points in the opposite direction, toward the policy-maker's assumptions of fact and affirmations of value, encouraging a growth of self-awareness relevant to the policy-maker's role. I review here the major components of such self-awareness.

Value

Consider again the question of educational potentials. If a child has not one but indefinitely many potentials of variable worth, if metaphysical essence does not provide an objective preselection among these, and if the total set always harbors internal conflict, the need for some independent selection becomes inescapable for the policy-maker. He or she must, in short, choose which to attempt to realize, which to minimize, counter, or ignore.

Of course, individuals working on policy matters typically work within an institutional framework. Policy does not issue from each person separately but usually represents the institution as a corporate product. In this respect, when speaking of "the policy-maker," I have in mind whatever agency is responsible for the policy product, whether individual or—as is more typically the case—institutional. The institution, as well as the individual, needs to become aware of its values, that is, its bases for selection of potentials to realize, by contrast with those it chooses to ignore or counteract. There is an institutional, as there is an individual, responsibility to make value criteria plain and to offer some rationale for them.

However, in emphasizing the powers of choice of individual agents, we have implicitly denied that such agents can altogether be relieved of responsibility for what they do, even when they work within an institution. The implication is that individuals ought to be reflective about the values of the policy-making institutions to which they contribute, by their work or otherwise. They need to insure that the contributions they make to the policy-making process command their own reflective assent.

Culture

A second component of self-awareness is *cultural context.* Here the point I emphasize relates not to the realization of potentials but to their very attribution, for in such attribution the assumed cultural context serves typically as a tacit parameter. Change the parameter and you may well change the very attribution; what one culture opens as a possibility for learning may be closed by another. This is an aspect of what might be termed the relativity of potential. Appreciation of such relativity should serve to draw the policy-maker's attention to his or her presuppositions as to cultural context.

That this point is of great importance in education may be seen by examining the role of denials of potential. Such denials function to absolve the policy-maker from accomplishing what is alleged to be impossible. If a child does *not have* the potential to become a skilled worker, or a professional, or a musician, or a writer, society surely cannot be charged with the obligation to realize such potential.

When the matter is left in this state, the issue is made to hinge simply on some feature of the child itself; the child is stigmatized as having a deficiency that stands in the way of a desirable outcome. The policy-maker is therefore free to turn his efforts elsewhere—to children *with,* rather than *without,* potential. Once, however, the allegedly critical feature of the child is understood to impede the outcome only *relatively* to presumed auxiliary conditions—for example, certain stereotypes as to race, sex, or socioeconomic class—the whole policy picture undergoes change. The deficiency is no longer assigned to the child alone but rather to the combination of child-and-context; "interactionism" replaces "essentialism."

Cross-cultural studies serve to alert us to the need to relativize our judgments of potential to conditions prevailing in our own culture. Finding, in particular, that certain achievements we had deemed generally precluded are in fact realized in some other society, we may withdraw or qualify our earlier generalization of incapacity. For reasons of this sort, if for no other, it is important that policy be informed by cross-cultural awareness, that policy-makers be encouraged to look at problems not solely in the context of their own societies, but also in the context of others remote in time, space, and character. Historical, anthropological, and comparative studies, in particular, ought to enter into the training of those involved in the formulation of principles governing educational efforts.

It may seem paradoxical that in advocating a greater measure of *self*-awareness on the part of policy-makers, I am here counseling a greater attention to *other* cultures. Yet there is here no paradox at all. Self-knowledge is a typical fruit of contrast with others, against which one's own distinctiveness is more sharply etched: this principle applies to groups as well as individuals. Historical and cross-cultural studies, which focus our attention on the customs, achievements, and values of other cultures, may thus bring about a new perception of our own distinctive values and assumptions.

Habit

I have discussed relativity to cultural context in a general way. Appreciation of such relativity, I have argued, alters the picture fundamentally, sensitizing us to possibilities otherwise excluded. But mere possibility, it may be countered, is not enough. The child is, after all, to be dealt with in his or her actual cultural context, not in some imagined alternative one. If the actual context is impervious to change by deliberate effort, it does not matter from a practical point of view that in hypothetically differing conditions the child's achievement might be quite different.

Here is where a third component of self-awareness becomes important, namely, an appreciation of the force of *habits and policies already established*. Policy issues arise in the context of habits and policies either already formed and functioning, or else in the process of being crystallized. The customs, habits, expectations, rules, operative programs, and presumptions that form the background of any question of policy are themselves principles of action of one sort or another. They are themselves of a piece with policy and, to varying degrees, often alterable by policy. They are, however, so much a part of the familiar environment that they are frequently not attended to as possible levers of change. But it is often the case that among the auxiliary conditions of a given impediment to achievement lie established modes of action accessible to deliberate alteration. Such alteration may, moreover, yield an alternative context for the child, overcoming the relevant hindrance.

That a child's disability blocks the achievement of a specific sort of learning, for example, may be true only if the available therapy or ameliorative technology is restricted in certain ways. That it is thus restricted may itself be the result of a policy or, at any rate, alterable by policy. Discriminatory treatment of poor or minority children that hampers their learning is not to be assumed to be an unalterable fact, inaccessible to policy initiatives. That the sort or level of schooling made available in a given region is inadequate for attaining certain learning outcomes may be a fact that is open to change by policy. Learning outcomes are affected critically by the allocation and distribution of resources established by prior policy. Throwing such policy itself into question rather than assuming it to be a fixed part of the cultural fabric may open the way to the educational outcomes in question.

Knowledge

A fourth component of the self-awareness we advocate for the policy-maker is that concerned with the state of knowledge. New knowledge may open the possibility of turning today's incapacity into tomorrow's capacity, thus enhancing potential, or it may open the prospect of doing just the reverse, and shrinking it.

We typically focus just on the enhancement of potential, but shrinkage is illustrated by the development of immunization procedures against certain diseases, thus destroying the undesirable potential of contracting these diseases. The will to destroy such potential was, in itself, obviously insufficient to do so prior to availability of the procedures. Without the procedures, it was more properly describable as a wish, or a hope, rather than a will; it reflected no policy option. The development of a vaccine against polio made possible for the first time an option of policy; it tested the social will to eliminate the disease.

Similarly, expansion of potential may follow upon new knowledge as to how to eliminate formerly preventive circumstances, or else how to alter the context so as to remove their preventive sting. A child afflicted with a physical disability may, for instance, be cured of it; alternatively, auxiliary devices may be supplied so that the disability no longer disables in the relevant respect. The supply of such devices is not an option prior to the development of the requisite knowledge; with such knowledge, it poses a new question for policy, putting the values as well as the will of society to the test.

A variety of distinctions relative to new knowledge must be borne in mind. Development of a new fundamental theory may be very far from pointing out some desirable action available to us. Therefore, it might not expand the effective range of our policy options no matter how significant it might otherwise be.

Even if the fundamental theory is applied so as to furnish the design principles for a relevant prosthetic device—say, to overcome a given disability—the production of such a device may still, as a practical matter, be far off. And production or supply, even if technically feasible, may still fall outside accepted or acceptable criteria of cost or desirability, that is to say, customary policies or reflective values. There is, in other words, a long way to be traversed between the creation of a new fundamental theory and the creation of a new, available action representing a policy alternative.

Nevertheless, the policy-maker needs to be aware of the continuum involved here, connecting theoretical knowledge in the abstract with actions falling within the range of present policy. The dynamic of fundamental research needs to be appreciated—its capacity eventually to impinge on practical options should not be underestimated. Conversely, it is important to see that problems *for* research are to be selected, at least partly, through identification of the practical problems to be solved.

While policy-makers ought to understand their field of action as alterable through knowledge, they ought also to recognize the autonomy of their role in pointing to problems of practice and in aiming to live up to a set of values and ideals. That knowledge changes the field of action should not be taken to mean that the translation of theory through technology into policy is inevitable. It is not the case that whatever *can* be done *should* be done. On the contrary, policy-makers need to exercise judgment throughout the continuum, exerting critical leverage on the future even as they execute present policy.

Policy-makers, finally, need to avoid the supposition that action is constrained by natural circumstances, independent of human knowledge. Human knowledge, itself a part of nature, transforms the rest of nature demonstrably and incalculably. To underestimate this power of ideas is not to be realistic but rather to be out of touch with reality. The point is not that ideas can do anything, nor is it that wishing will make it so, but rather that what is predictable, permissible, or preventable is not a function of nature to the exclusion of human knowledge and effort.

The geographical setting of a historical episode certainly exercises an important influence on its course, yet it is not possible to specify this influence independently of the state of current knowledge. What harder physical facts could there be, after all, then mountain ranges and distances? Nevertheless, as Frederick Olafson points out,

> the geography in question is human geography, that is, those features of the natural setting that block or facilitate human effort in one or another

of its major areas. Those features of the natural setting have to be described because they stand in some relationship to human need and effort; and they assume their full significance in a historical account only when they are set in the context of a certain level of technology and technological capabilities. Thus, distances have a quite different meaning for purposes of sixteenth-century history than for twentieth-century history because the "coefficient of adversity" they present is specifiable only for a stipulated level of technology. All too often this interdependence of natural setting and human activity has been forgotten or left implicit in the geographical sections of history books.[6]

The moral is that the policy-maker needs to look not only outward but inward, taking due account not only of "external" circumstances but of those circumstances as interacting with available or likely knowledge and technology.

Policy and Time

I have advocated a multidisciplinary approach to problems of practice, urging that policy-makers integrate the results of special inquiries bearing on common problems. I have also emphasized conceptual and valuational issues. But special note should be taken of the need for a historical sense— an appreciation of the temporal dimension of policy. I shall now address five questions relating to this dimension, turning first to the question of continuity.

Potentials and Continuity

In solving a mechanical problem, an engineer takes account of the momentary configuration of bodies and the momentary disposition of variable physical forces, but that hardly turns engineering into history. Policy-makers, similarly, acknowledge temporal variation in the factors that concern them, but they typically maintain an engineering rather than a historical attitude toward their subject matter. As the focus of policy is, in any case, on what is to be done now with the resources available, the emphasis is on the foreground, not the background, and the attitude is practical rather than reminiscent or speculative. The policy-maker may be keenly sensitive to novel opportunity and, in this sense, alert to the ripening of time, yet fundamentally ahistorical in his or her general consciousness.

Nor does developmentalism of the Piagetian variety supply the historical sense I have in mind. For such developmentalism postulates the ordered emergence of forms of thought in the child, under specified conditions, as a general fact of growth. It provides an abstract schema of change, focusing on certain formal aspects of mental capacity and discerning a uniform pattern in their emergence. But it does not purport to offer an account of the continuity of educational growth bridging "form" and "content," peculiar to certain children but not all, and extending beyond the limited course of stages postulated. It describes no particular path through time but, in effect, asserts a set of general laws governing the rise of certain mental capacities.

What is wanted is a concept of continuity, a tracing of the individual path of a child's growth and education, and an idea of alternative paths that might be followed, given appropriate actions and auxiliary conditions. The waxing and waning of educational potentials over time, their variation with realization, the interplay of realization with motivation and subsequent learning—all these and still other educational factors may be integrated into a relatively continuous account of growth, both as it has already occurred and as it may occur in the future.

Selfhood and Temporal Integration

Why is the possibility of such a continuous account important for the policy-maker? It is important because he or she is dealing with people, not objects. Although objects are spread out in time just as people are, they have no conception of themselves as spread out in time. Their temporal features may be of interest to us, but they do not enter into self-conceptions of the objects themselves, partially determining their future histories. On the other hand, people are not only extended in time, but understand themselves as thus extended, forming their self-conceptions through rootedness in a past conserved in memory, and through directedness toward a future guided by aspiration. The child's conception of its own potentials is not an isolated thing, cut off from such temporal integration. Its growing powers reflect and stimulate a growing sense of self, and the exercise of such powers closely meshes with developing motivation and adult purpose. The organization of a person's life is a continuity sought across time.

The perception of such continuity in the lives touched by educational policy carries inestimable significance for the policy-maker. The child who comes to school for the first time is continuous in self-conception with the earlier child of family, neighborhood, and community. Such continuity requires sensitive acknowledgment by schools. It is not only intrinsically proper that teachers strive to appreciate the backgrounds of their pupils—especially those who differ from them in culture, class, race, religion, or native tongue. There is an educational point as well. The memories and aspirations of the child, continuous with the memories and aspirations of its family and community, are threads along which educational matter will crystallize, even as these threads themselves undergo change.

Moreover, the school's own program of studies must strive for temporal integration. Often the topic of integration in the curriculum is treated as if it concerned only the synchronous bridging of the various subjects, with scant attention given to bridging across time. But the educational life of the child is continuous. It should not be viewed as segmented into the temporal bits sanctioned by local school practice. Nor should the schooling of children be construed as exhausting the temporal limits of education, continuous in fact throughout the whole course of a person's life. To recognize the temporal continuity of education is, in sum, a major desideratum of policy.

Connectivity of Policy Decisions

Aside from continuity in the lives of those affected by their policies, policy-makers need to come to terms with the continuity of their own actions. Their decisions have a temporal dimension no less important than that of the persons they influence. They stand within the same stream of time and are subject to the same drive for self-consistency and temporal continuity. Acknowledging these aspects of the policy-maker's role is another, and equally important, way of embodying a historical awareness.

Policy is not a matter of solving one problem and then, having wiped the slate clean, addressing the next. Each solution leaves its traces, to be felt as part of the subsequent problem that must be faced. Such traces may, more-over, be anticipated to a greater or lesser degree, and with varying reliability: if one of several alternative actions is taken now, where will it lead and what decisional alternatives will it open up? And assuming that such and such conditions arise at that time, what may then be expected as a likely outcome, and what decisions might then be available as options? The action to be taken at this moment is to be taken in the light of linked expectations of this sort.

The basis of such expectations is the record of past experience coupled with a shrewd analysis of present circumstances. Policy decision, like all action as I have earlier described it, involves both memory and imagination, judging some present course to be an optimal pathway to the future, in light of some recalled past. In this respect, policy is a species of time-binding, like all action. However, because it is a public function, its rationale and evidence need to be made as explicit as possible.

Judgment underlies policy, and judgment implies discrimination: some assumptions are better than others, some are plausible, some positively discredited. As just suggested, the basis of judgment is some recalled past. It is crucially important, however, to avoid fastening upon isolated past instances as evidence for policy assumptions. In using the past as guide to the present, critical analysis of the available evidence is what is needed.

Policy-Making and Policy Testing

An implication of this critical attitude is that the consequences of a prior decision require scrutiny as they continue to occur, since they not only set the scene for further action but test the assumptions made earlier. Such testing contributes to the improvement of future decision-making by weeding out the falsified assumptions that are still operative in policy thinking. Learning from experience is thus a matter of retaining a memory of the beliefs underlying a past judgment and utilizing its present outcomes to check these beliefs. If policy-making is to improve through learning from experience, it must not only look forward to the future but also backward to the past. The role of the policy-maker, construed critically, involves not simply the making of decisions for the future but also the checking of past decisions by monitoring their presently discernible outcomes. Thus the policy-maker not only shapes policy but may also contribute to its improvement.

This critical role is exceedingly difficult to realize. It requires a double consciousness, demanding energetic fulfillment of commitments already undertaken, while at the same time demanding a skeptical reserve vis-à-vis assumptions underlying these very commitments—a deference to accumulating evidence, a willingness to concede, if such evidence so indicates, that these assumptions may, after all, have been mistaken and, therefore, that the policies were perhaps wrong.

Not only is the mere "doubling" of consciousness a hardship; the two attitudes seem to be in conflict. Once a policy is undertaken, the energies, reputations, and egos of its agents become invested in it to a greater or lesser degree. The possibility that it may be wrong is experienced as a threat to the self. Psychological forces are mobilized to defend the self through vigorous defense of the policy in question. Defensiveness, denial, and wishful thinking tend to take over and thwart critical analysis. Conversely, a cool, skeptical reserve, a wait-and-see attitude pending the evidence, a continuing survey of alternatives to present policy—all these tend to blunt commitment and delay action, and, in extreme cases, to postpone action indefinitely in favor of further scrutiny of the evidence from the safe vantage point of the ivory tower.

This conflict of attitudes poses the most serious threat to the life of policy, for it polarizes the alternatives and presents us with an impossible choice: either execute policy decisions with total and unthinking commitment or else refrain from action altogether. In either case, the improvement of policy through learning from experience is ruled out completely, since such learning requires both a continuing audit of past experience and a continuous commitment to act upon the future.

Luckily, the conflict of attitudes in question is nothing like a logical contradiction. There is no purely *logical* bar to the combination of resolute action with critical intelligence; nor is there any natural law forbidding all but dogmatists to act and all but passive persons to reason. What is sorely needed, however, is institutional ingenuity applied to the problem of relating decision and criticism—or, put more generally, theory and practice—in the realm of policy.

Policy-making and policy execution need to be constantly monitored to insure that continuing criticism and testing feed back into ongoing activity. The education of policy-makers ought, moreover, to inform their professional selves with the twin values of resoluteness under uncertainty, and the redirection of such resoluteness with changing evidence.

What the wise physician does both in providing definite therapy and in critically revising such provision in light of new evidence is what the policy-maker needs to do. He or she should feel obliged to offer, at each juncture, the guidance best warranted by contemporaneous evidence. In striving to do so, the policy-maker may take pride both in active practice and in the welcoming of changes in such practice indicated by the evidence. Criticism of his or her past practice is no longer necessarily a threat, nor does it in any way suggest that practice is to be shunned in the future. But reconceiving the policy role as a critical one is, of course, not simply a matter of realigning the policy-maker's attitudes; it involves changes, as well, in the institutional and attitudinal setting within which policy functions.

Policy, Norm, and Community

A further focus of historical awareness is important in considering the policy-maker's role. It concerns not the decision or the decision chain itself, as solution to some problem of practice, but rather the ramifications of decision into norm and precedent. For every decision inevitably reverberates outward, spills beyond the bounds of the problem, no matter how initially conceived. It creates precedents, activates analogies with the past, helps to form, strengthen, or modify a general style, a set of norms that newly influence criteria of consistency in action. Choices generalize, with or without the help of words; all decisions are "decisions of principle."[7]

Critical problem-solving is thus by no means the only element of importance requiring reference to past experience. Actions, pointed toward particular ends, are at one and the same time systematic in their significance. In striving to accomplish their ends, they simultaneously strengthen or attenuate a received style of striving, legitimate and embody a type of precedent, reinforce or re-create the normative space in which they were conceived.

This normative space is a vehicle of self-identity, both for the individual and the community. It imposes a broad presumptive pattern on our further action, thus promoting the sense of our durable agency. Our actions ought, then, to be examined not only for clues to their effectiveness, but for a sense of the normative space they help to form. We need to ask not just what success our decisions have brought but what precedents they have wrought; not just what we have done to transform the problem but how our deeds have transformed ourselves.

This picture applies both to the individual and to the community. But policy, in the normal usage of the term, has to do with the community in particular, expressing, indeed comprising, the action of a community. Those with the authority to make and execute policies carry others with them along a certain historical path, at least presumptively. The maxims underlying policy typically refer, moreover, to community interests with considerably longer time-spans than the individual life, and they invite coordinated efforts across the generations. Think, for example, of the political interests of nations or the doctrinal orientations of religious associations. Policy thus reflects, and reacts upon, the long-range time-binding of historical communities, possessed of common memories and shared dreams for the future. It is within the medium of such communities, partially shaped by policy, that individual efforts are conducted, individual lives planned, individual choices made. It is because this impact of policy is so pervasive that the historical awareness I have urged is of fundamental importance.

Notes

1. On related points, see Joseph J. Schwab, *Science, Curriculum, and Liberal Education,* ed. Ian Westbury and Niel J. Wilkof (Chicago: University of Chicago Press, 1978), in particular, his papers on the practical, pp. 287–385. Schwab emphasizes the partiality of the special disciplines and the need to promote an "inclination toward and competence for examining educational situations and problems in more than one set of terms" (p. 356). For discussion of some of Schwab's views, see Chapter 16 of my *Reason and Teaching* (Indianapolis, Ind.: Hackett, 1973).

2. See Scheffler, *Reason and Teaching,* pp. 54–56.

3. As Schwab says, "The vice is tunnel vision. The possessor of only one of a collection of competing theories sees its subject matter in only the peculiar light cast by that theory." *Science, Curriculum, and Liberal Education,* p. 333.

4. See, for discussion of this theme in connection with the teacher's role, Scheffler, *Reason and Teaching,* chap. 5.

5. For discussion of teleological explanation, see my *The Anatomy of Inquiry* (New York: Knopf, 1963: Indianapolis, Ind.: Hackett, 1981), pp. 76–123; and C. G. Hempel, *Aspects of Scientific Explanation* (New York: Free Press, 1975), pp. 254–56, 303–4, and 325–29. A recent comprehensive treatment of teleological explanation in the context of philosophy of history is presented in F. A. Olafson, *The Dialectic of Action* (Chicago: University of Chicago Press. 1979).

6. Olafson, *The Dialectic of Action,* p. 140.

7. The phrase is R. M. Hare's. See his *The Language of Morals* (New York: Clarendon Press, Oxford University, 1952), pp. 56–78.

11

Four Languages of Education

I. Introduction: Many Disciplines, One Profession

I have long held that educational study does not comprise a single discipline but incorporates several disciplines. In *The Language of Education* (1960) I wrote: "Educational research must not be conceived as a single science, but rather as the common focus of many sciences with bearings on educational practice. These sciences include not only psychology but also, for example, sociology, anthropology, biology, and economics."[1]

In a later paper I argued against the idea that a "special discipline of education"[2] is needed as a foundation for professional identity. On the contrary, I urged, as educators, "we ought not to isolate ourselves from attempts to formulate principles relevant to our own work, no matter what their disciplinary labels. . . . Rather, we should encourage relevant investigations by psychologists, anthropologists, sociologists, economists, educationalists, and still others, and we should strive to link them with the concerns of schooling. There is surely enough substance in such an enterprise to support a genuine and important professional identity."[3]

II. Practical Theory and Professional Practice

In my *Of Human Potential*[4] I returned to this theme and elaborated it, emphasizing not just the diversity of scientific disciplines but also the importance of other elements of belief in the equipment of the professional. Following a suggestion of P. H. Hirst,[5] I now used the term "practical theory," as distinct from "scientific theory," to refer to the composite set of beliefs that guide the practices of any given profession. I contrasted these two terms as follows:

Presented as a lecture at the University of Padua in 1987. Translated into Italian by Francesca Gobbo of the University of Padua, it appeared as "I quattro linguaggi dell' educazione," *Studi de Storia dell' Educazione* 8, no. 1 (1988): 70–77.

"A scientific theory is a law-like statement or set of statements, formulated in the vocabulary of a scientific discipline, which claims to give a truthful representation of the phenomena studied by the discipline. A scientific theory is judged by its contribution to the understanding of such phenomena; in practice, it is assessed by its logical coherence, its explanatory power, and its heuristic fruitfulness, as judged by the methodological canons of the discipline. Science tends toward increasing systematization of theory and progressive abstractness of vocabulary. In its drive toward ever more comprehensive explanation, its theories comprise increasingly autonomous and integrated structures, with constituent terms departing further and further from the familiar language of everyday practical experience. The organization of theoretical knowledge within a scientific discipline is, in short, dictated by the twin aims of general understanding and the further growth of such understanding.

"A practical theory, by contrast, organizes its propositions so as to provide guidance to some practical enterprise, for example, the healing of the sick, the construction of shelters, the rearing of the young. In the professions associated with these enterprises, namely, medicine, engineering, and education, we have primary examples of such differing organization. The knowledge relevant to any one of these professions is drawn from no single scientific discipline. A variety of disciplines, rather, must be presupposed in typical professional work, the practical problems addressed being unconstrained by the limits of any single one and spilling over into each.

"Moreover, beyond every disciplinary account available, there are elements of knowledge and value that enter into all professional activity. There is, first of all, knowledge of an array of problems as they present themselves in relevant contexts of practice rather than contexts of inquiry. The patient feels pain or cannot walk; the bridge sways or is too narrow to accommodate rush-hour traffic; the child is having difficulty reading. Each of these descriptions is couched, not in the specialized language of a discipline, but in the idiom of everyday life. Each expresses, not a law-like generalization, but the character of a situation affecting human beings who are disposed to notice and respond to it in one way or another, even if not by overt action. Such expressions, in whatever language is natural to the persons in question, are essential to identifying the problems that professions must treat. They form part of the practical theory underlying a profession.

"Second, professions are governed by distinctive purposes defining their scope and limits. The basic knowledge of the physician can be used to poison as well as to heal, but the ethics of medicine is not neutral on this question, forbidding the one and enjoining the other. A profession embodies comprehensive values respecting the problematic choices falling within its purview. Statements of such values and associated principles of action are indispensable constituents of its practical theory.

"The organization of a practical theory is dictated, not by the aim of advancing general understanding, but by the effort to guide decision in some realm of practice. It is the practical questions of such a realm which provide the common focus for the elements of its practical theory. From a purely disciplinary point of view, such a theory is composite, inelegant, roughly hewn. But for the purpose it is meant to serve in guiding practical judgment, a composite account is clearly more functional than a purely disciplinary theory would be. Who would choose to ride over a bridge whose builder knew only theoretical physics but nothing about the stresses of available materials or the local functions to be served by the bridge? Who would elect a surgeon who knew only biochemistry, or only physiology, or only anatomy, but nothing about other relevant disciplines or the patient's history or the success rate of the surgical procedure in question? Aside from the clinical training and experience of the aspiring professional, his theoretical education must surely be understood as composite if it is to be effective. For it is the task of the professional to draw together the understandings achieved by relevant disciplines and to apply them, under the guidance of an ethical ideal, to the problems of ordinary experience."[6]

Starting with this conception of the practical theory of education, I shall now proceed to distinguish four sorts of language encountered in the profession, and thus requiring acknowledgement in its practical theory. I call these sorts: (a) *the technical;* (b) *the narrative;* (c) *the evaluative;* and (d) *the pedagogical.* In the remainder of my presentation, I will explain and comment on each sort.

III. Technical Language and its Logic

Much special knowledge bearing upon education is now available and more is becoming available each day. Such knowledge is often technical in the sense that it is developed within a scientific discipline of inquiry, involving methods of analysis and canons of evaluation peculiar to that discipline. Knowledge relating, for example, to nutrition, neurology, linguistics, psychology, and cognitive science may be considered technical in this sense. The educator obviously cannot be expected to master all these special fields and other related fields as well. Still, if he is to judge a proposed application of such knowledge to education, he requires at least a modicum of the relevant technical background.

But more than technique is required of the educator. In particular, he needs to be able to question the researcher intelligently, and this implies an understanding of the general structure of research. For if technical items, such as mathematical formulas, theoretical constructs, and special notations, are to be properly applied, their logical bases and methodological rationales have to be comprehended. What functions do such items serve in inquiry, what is their conceptual basis and their empirical warrant, what limits on their interpretation are presupposed? Intelligent use of special knowledge requires a grasp of its underlying logic.

To be avoided above all is the notion that technical results are hard-and-fast truths, to be accepted by the educator without question and applied directly to educational practice in whatever ways may seem plausible. On the contrary, the educator must insist that the scope and meaning of every such result is qualified by its logical and methodological context. He certainly need not, and cannot, become a specialist in every discipline relevent to his work. But he can and should be equipped to raise critical questions addressed to the specialists, concerning their basic concepts and the logic of their argumentation.

The educator needs, further, to be prepared to integrate the practical considerations that seem to flow from diverse disciplines of research, for example, from psychology, sociology, and organizational development. The architect, to take an example from a different profession, must similarly deal with and relate the economic, physical, and sociological bearings of his design. Such integration is not given within any single discipline. It is not itself a further disciplinary specialty, but rather a matter of experienced judgment and professional art. It requires a sensitivity to the languages and procedures of diverse special inquiries and an ability to link them, applying them conjointly in applications to practice.

IV. Narrative Language and Human Problems

To apply the special results of science to educational problems presupposes that these problems are independently specifiable. Such problems, like all problems of practice, arise not in a segregated domain ordered for the purpose of inquiry by a given discipline, but rather in the fullness of everyday life, the scene of multiple human activities, experiences, purposes, and needs. The awareness of such problems is not the monopoly of any special discipline, nor the exclusive province of any set of disciplines. Pooling the specialized perspectives of the several forms of inquiry does not yet guarantee human understanding. Such understanding, addressed to the activities and feelings of people, requires access to the way those people understand themselves; it requires that they be heard when they speak in their own voice.

Typically, what they say takes the form of a story told in the first person, or it can readily be put into that form. The physician thus takes a history from the patient in the patient's own language; the psychologist or psychiatrist composes a case study based at least in part on the patient's self-reports. By the notion of "a story" in the present context, I wish to emphasize not merely that particular occurrences are narrated in a chronological sequence but also—and particularly—that the sequence is structured by the narrator's intention. That is to say, it is the narrator's view of things that governs the story's development, the narrator's beliefs, desires, obstacles, and lacks that frame its dramatic movement, and the narrator's vocabulary that shapes the episodes recounted and defines the current problem to be faced.

Narrative language, as I use this phrase, thus discloses to the professional how a problem looks to the person whose problem it is. The narration helps the professional to focus his disciplinary equipment, to relate it appropriately to the human beings whose problems need attention. If the narration is to serve in this way, it must be taken seriously by the professional, although it lies altogether outside the framework of his disciplinary discourse. He must sharpen his capacity to listen and to comprehend the discourse of his client. The educator, in sum, should be multilingual, not only with respect to the several disciplines of inquiry, but also with respect to the ordinary languages of those people whose problems such inquiry addresses. For the very relevance of disciplinary findings is intrinsically affected by the meanings such people may place on them.[7]

V. Evaluative Language and the Autonomy of the Educator

Every profession is guided by a special set of values defining its purpose and its proper mode of operation. Its presumed knowledge base in empirical inquiries, and its practical skills, are not sufficient to define its identity. For empirical knowledge and practical proficiency can both be used for good or for ill, whereas a profession must be understood as guided peculiarly by benevolent or altruistic values. An engineer who is not *able* to build a collapsible bridge is incompetent, but an engineer who *will* build such a bridge is immoral. Both competence and ethical character are required in every profession, and it is indeed the twin presumptions of competence and character upon which the profession bases its claim on society's trust and support. Moreover, it cannot establish its claim once and for all; it has to earn its position of trust by a continuous process of reviewing, testing, and advancing its knowledge and skill, and by a continuing effort to monitor its conduct in the light of its fundamental values.

If the profession depends on the trust of society, it also, however, reserves the right to instruct and to criticize social practice. Commitment to basic professional values provides a rationale for such autonomy. The educator qua educator, for example, is bound by his defining values. His role is not merely to pursue with maximal efficiency goals that are independently determined; he is not merely a "minor technician"[8] at the beck and call of society. Rather, his professional commitment to the ideals of truth, understanding, scholarly integrity, and respect for persons allows him to speak with an independent voice to the very society that supports his special status within it. Committed to such ideals, the educator cannot stand aloof from issues of social policy, taking refuge in the role of disciplinary expert or pedagogical craftsman. He stands not outside the realm of value but squarely within it.

Accelerating social change renders the value problems of education ever more complex and pressing. To take one urgent example, the revolution in communications and computer technology opens radically new possibilities for the conduct of the learning process. Whether—and if so, how—these possibilities ought to be realized in schooling, however, is a question of social choice, the outcome of which is by no means predetermined. If educators are not simply to adopt a passive attitude in the face of these possibilities, they need to investigate them from an educational point of view, raising not only questions of effectiveness but also questions of value—ends as well as means.[9]

A willingness to engage in considerations of this sort requires a degree of fluency in the use of evaluative language. Such language is of course not the special province of professionals; it belongs to all of us. But it is, in any case, of the first importance for those professionally dedicated as spokesmen for the fundamental values of education.[10]

VI. Pedagogical Language and the Range of Symbolism

Pedagogical contexts call for the educator's language to promote the student's learning. Obviously, there is no single form of language uniquely effective for this purpose. Clearly, also, pedagogical language encompasses the sorts I have so far distinguished. Thus, teachers employ technical language in the teaching of science and mathematics, narrative language in classes on literature and history, and evaluative language in courses on civics or in moral education.

What I want to call attention to here, however, is a further form of language that, although apparently inferior to literally accurate technical language, surpasses it in pedagogical achievement. Examples abound in the training of skills and performance, whether in sports or in the arts, but are by no means restricted to these spheres.

Certainly, in these as well as other areas, pedagogical utterances may be issued primarily to motivate and monitor correct responses rather than to describe; thus the teacher will say things to the student to encourage or discourage, to approve or disapprove, to praise or to blame. But the sort of language I have in mind is clearly descriptive and not merely motivational or expressive.

Thus, the literally false—indeed impossible—instructions by a voice coach to a student, "Sing from the top of your head," "Sing with an inner smile," or "Sing as if you were smelling a rose" may be pedagogically effective, whereas a literally accurate physiological descriptive of what is wanted would not.[11]

The more general point is that the literally accurate scientific explanation is not in general transposable into effective pedagogy. By contrast, the metaphorical lore of the craft may in fact be pedagogically superior, having been selected in part for its usefulness in the training of novices.

The language of effective pedagogy follows its own route, irreplaceable by other forms and deserving respectful study in its own right. Rather than being derivative from science, such language challenges science to describe its functioning and explain why it works. Indeed, having come this far, we must break the bonds of language itself in order to encompass other symbolic devices effective in pedagogy, e.g., demonstrations, directive gestures, sketches, pictures, diagrams, graphs, caricatures, rituals, models—all beyond words but indispensable instruments of education. A study of such instruments yields a broadening of our conception of thought itself—coincident with a wide variety of symbolic functioning.[12]

Notes

1. I. Scheffler, *The Language of Education* (Springfield, Ill.: Charles Thomas, 1960), p. 73.

2. I. Scheffler, "Is Education a Discipline?" (1961), reprinted in *Reason and Teaching* (London: Routledge & Kegan Paul, 1973), p. 48.

3. Ibid., pp. 55–56.

4. I. Scheffler, *Of Human Potential* (London: Routledge & Kegan Paul, 1985).

5. P. H. Hirst, "Philosophy and Educational Theory," *British Journal of Educational Studies* 12 (1963): 51–64. On the relation of disciplines to educational practice, see my "Is Education a Discipline?" in *Reason and Teaching*. On application of disciplines to practice, see Joseph J. Schwab, *Science, Curriculum, and Liberal Education*, ed. I. Westbury and N. J. Wilkof (Chicago: University of Chicago Press, 1978), esp. pt. 3.

6. Scheffler, *Of Human Potential*, pp. 5–6.

7. Related themes are treated in *Of Human Potential*, esp. chap. 4. On narration and intention, in the context of the philosophy of history, see F. A. Olafson, *The Dialectic of Action* (Chicago: The University of Chicago Press, 1979). On the recent use of "portraiture" in the description of educational institutions and processes, see Sara Lawrence Lightfoot, *The Good High School* (New York: Basic Books, 1983).

8. Scheffler, *Reason and Teaching*, p. 61.

9. For general discussion of this issue, see I. Scheffler, "Computers at School?" *Teachers College Record* 87 (1986): 513–28.

10. See R. S. Peters, *Ethics and Education* (London: Allen & Unwin, 1970).

11. For these and related examples, see V. A. Howard, *Artistry: The Work of Artists* (Indianapolis, Ind.: Hackett, 1982).

12. See Nelson Goodman, *Languages of Art* (Indianapolis, Ind.: Hackett, 1968); C. Elgin, *With Reference to Reference* (Indianapolis, Ind.: Hackett, 1983); D. Perkins and B. Leondar, *The Arts and Cognition* (Baltimore, Md.: Johns Hopkins Press, 1977); V. A. Howard, *Artistry*; and I. Scheffler, *Inquiries* (Indianapolis, Ind.: Hackett, 1986, pt. 1, chaps. 6 and 7).

12

Vice Into Virtue, or Seven Deadly Sins of Education Redeemed

Introduction

My purpose in what follows is to reveal some of the virtues hidden in what are typically deemed unqualified educational vices. I am encouraged in this purpose by one of William James's celebrated *Talks to Teachers,* in which he urged his hearers not to disparage passions "often . . . considered unworthy . . . to appeal to in the young," but rather to redirect them to good educational use, "reaping [their] advantages . . . in such a way as to [achieve] a maximum of benefit with a minimum of harm." Thus, as against Rousseau, who, in his *Emile,* had attacked the use of rivalry as a motive in education, James defended "the feeling of rivalry" as "[lying] at the very basis of our being, all social improvement being largely due to it. There is a noble and generous kind of rivalry," James wrote, "as well as a spiteful and greedy kind; and the noble and generous form is particularly common in childhood. All games owe the zest which they bring with them to the fact that they are rooted in the emulous passion, yet they are the chief means of training in fairness and magnanimity. Can the teacher afford to throw such an ally away?"[1]

Similarly, James defended appeal to the pupil's pride and pugnacity since "in their more refined and noble forms they play a great part in the schoolroom and in education generally, being in some characters most potent spurs to effort. Pugnacity," he continued,

> need not be thought of merely in the form of physical combativeness. It can be taken in the sense of a general unwillingness to be beaten by any kind of difficulty. It is what makes us feel "stumped" and challenged by arduous achievements, and is essential to a spirited and enterprising character. . . . It is nonsense to suppose that every step in education *can*

Presented 25 April 1989 at Framingham State College, as part of its Sesquicentennial Celebration. Reprinted from *Teachers College Record* 91, no. 2 (1989): 177 – 89.

be interesting. The fighting impulse must often be appealed to. Make the pupil feel ashamed of being scared at fractions, of being "downed" by the law of falling bodies; rouse his pugnacity and pride, and he will rush at the difficult places with a sort of inner wrath at himself that is one of his best moral faculties. . . . The teacher who never rouses this sort of pugnacious excitement in his pupils falls short of one of his best forms of usefulness.[2]

And, to take my final example, James had warm words for the sense of ownership, which he considered "also one of the radical endowments of the race." This sense, he wrote, "begins in the second year of life. Among the first words which an infant learns to utter are the words 'my' and 'mine' and woe to the parents of twins who fail to provide their gifts in duplicate." Private proprietorship James considered to be part of human nature, it being "essential to mental health that the individual should have something beyond the bare clothes on his back to which he can assert exclusive possession, and which he may defend adversely against the world."

> Even those religious orders who makes the most stringent vows of poverty have found it necessary to relax the rule a little in favor of the human heart made unhappy by reduction to too disinterested terms. The monk must have his books; the nun must have her little garden, and the images and pictures in her room.[3]

In education, said James, ownership "can be appealed to in many ways" notably "in connection with one of its special forms of activity, the collecting impulse." Much of scholarship indeed, rests on "bibliography, memory and erudition," and in these aspects owes its interest to "the collecting instinct" rather than "to our cravings after rationality":

> A man wishes a complete collection of information, wishes to know more about a subject than anybody else, much as another may wish to own more dollars or more early editions . . . than anybody else.
> The teacher who can work this impulse into the school tasks is fortunate. Almost all children collect something. A tactful teacher may get them to take pleasure in collecting books; in keeping a neat and orderly collection of notes; in starting, when they are mature enough, a card catalogue; in preserving every drawing or map which they make. Neatness, order, and method are thus instinctively gained, along with the other benefits which the possession of the collection entails.[4]

In showing how rivalry, pugnacity, and ownership can be put to good use, James provokes us to reevaluate these motives. They are not to be denied or disparaged as such, but rather prized as potential instruments of teaching. Viewed as James invites us to view them, they are transformed from debits into assets, from obstacles into opportunities, from vices into potential virtues. The naive aversion they typically inspire is now seen to have been misguided; overcoming such aversion yields an enhancement of educational effectiveness.

Now James's idea of extracting the good from the presumptively bad can be applied well beyond the sphere of motives, to include educational states or processes generally. In what follows, I have selected seven of these for discussion. They are in such bad repute as to be popularly deemed vices— it is perhaps no exaggeration to say that they are regarded as the seven deadly sins of education. I will argue, to the contrary, that they are neither sinful nor deadly in themselves—nor are they vicious. Rather, when properly qualified, they constitute educational goods, to be wisely promoted or exploited by the sensitive teacher. These seven are ignorance, negativity, forgetting, guesswork, irrelevance, procrastination, and idleness.

I begin first with ignorance.

I. Ignorance, or What We Don't Know

There is a quatrain that used to be circulated, concerning the great nineteenth-century classicist and educator Benjamin Jowett, Master of Balliol College, Oxford, that went like this:

> My name is Benjamin Jowett
> If there is any knowledge I know it
> I am the Master of Balliol College
> If I don't know it, it's not knowledge.

The ideal represented in this quatrain is not only an ancient one but one that still reigns in education. It is knowledge that is thought to be the be-all and end-all of education, the gaining of fact and the eradication of ignorance. Knowledge, after all, is what education has to convey, the justification of schooling and the raison d'être of the teacher. Far from tempering this hoary conception, the momentum of our computer age with its associated notions of information, databases, and the knowledge explosion serves only to entrench it still further in the public mind.

One flaw in this idea is its suggestion that the matter of education is available in advance; that schooling is simply the process of conveying it to pupils. John Stuart Mill, in a scathing comment of 1832 on the education of his day, characterized such education as "all *cram.* . . . The world already knows everything, and has only to tell it to its children."[5] In its popular modern dress, the idea is that all the important information is already in the database, the pupil needing only computer literacy to enable him or her to retrieve it at will.[6]

A related defect is the confusion of *knowing* with the acquisition of *knowledge*, i.e., reliable information. To know a proposition expressing a bit of information is, however, more than just to have accepted it. It is to have earned the right to accept it, through a grasp of its meaning and warrant. Knowledge as a collective heritage of recorded information is indeed a fundamental resource of the teacher, but it cannot be transferred bit by bit in growing accumulation within the student's mind. The teacher must strive rather to promote an insight into the meaning, basis, and use of this collective heritage, so that the student may in fact come to know it rather than simply being informed of it. But even such knowing is not enough to express the aims of education, for it leaves out the opportunity for *innovation* by the learner, his ability to go beyond a knowing of available truths. We do not feed into the learner's mind all that we hope he will have as an end result of our teaching. We do *not* already know everything; our pupils can and should be expected to gain new understandings beyond our present grasp, they will need to revise our science, expand and modify our scholarship, recast our social, historical, and legal suppositions. They will, in short, need to discover new truths beyond our ken and reshape the very heritage of knowledge we now teach them.[7]

It is here that the importance of acknowledging our ignorance can be clearly seen. To educate our pupils for innovation in the world of the future they will inhabit, we evidently cannot *give* them the new truths they will need, for such truths in the nature of the case are unavailable to us; they lie beyond our grasp. If we had them to give, they would not be new. What we *can* do is to avoid giving our pupils the idea that our heritage is a seamless web of settled facts, an idea that is not only false but intimidates the adventurous spirit and chills the impulse of inquiry.

The plain fact is that this heritage of ours has gaps and fissures, jagged edges and incomplete contours. Our science contains contradictions and enigmas, our philosophy deep difficulties and disagreements. It is not just that there is much we do not yet know. It is that we positively know our knowledge to be faulty. Our ignorance is not simply privative—indicating a lack—but throbbingly assertive. No one has expressed better the precarious nature of our heritage than Michael Oakeshott, who describes it in these words:

> This inheritance is an historic achievement, . . . it is contingent upon circumstances, it is miscellaneous and incoherent; it is what human beings have achieved, not by the impulsion of a final cause, but by exploiting the opportunities of fortune and by means of their own efforts. . . . It does not deliver to us a clear and unambiguous message; it speaks often in riddles; it offers us advice and suggestion, recommendations, aids to reflection, rather than directives. It has been put together, not by designers but by men who knew only dimly what they did.[8]

Acquiring such an inheritance is described by Oakeshott as "leaning how to participate in a conversation: it is at once initiation into an inheritance in which we have a life interest, and the exploration of its intimations."[9]

The further point I would emphasize is that the gaps, difficulties, and riddles in our heritage are not educational obstacles to be minimized or deplored. They are in fact inspirational to the learner. They tell him that there are things he is called upon to do—intimations to explore, enigmas to resolve, conflicts to overcome, revisions to effect, new paths to discover. Ignorance, thus interpreted, is not a mere void but an infinite space rich with educational possibilities to beckon the active young mind. Far from being an embarrassment, ignorance should be given a proud and central place in our curricula.

Socrates claimed to be the wisest of men only because, although he knew nothing, he also knew that he knew nothing. I do not take matters to that extreme. There are plenty of things we do know, but what we know is precarious, gappy, enormously limited, and problematic. It is these aspects of our knowledge that should be made explicit and salient in our teaching.

II. Negativity, or The Power of Negative Thinking

Positive thinking is much overrated. There is, for example, a prevalent myth that science builds its theories on positive results. But a theory is false if it fails anywhere, no matter how many positive results it yields. Superstitions are false not because they lack positive instances but because they also have negative ones; they are believed because we fasten on the former and conveniently repress the latter. As Karl Popper has emphasized, we ought not praise a theory simply because it has positive instances. A theory needs, further, to withstand our most strenuous efforts to overthrow it. It is the mark of science not that it seeks to confirm its theories but rather that it seeks to disconfirm them through experimental test, hunting for whatever negative instances they may harbor.[10]

Negative thinking shows its power not only in the testing of ideas but also in their generation. New ideas thrive in the imagination, which negates what is and ponders what might be. Without the capacity to eliminate the positive and accentuate the negative, to skirt the actual and explore the possible, we would be forever captives of the past. Nothing is more important in education than finding ways to cultivate the imagination, the power to negate actualities in thought and leave pious pedantries behind.

Several years ago two former colleagues of mine, Stephen Brown and Marion Walter, worked out a way of teaching mathematics that has, ever since, exemplified for me the possibilities of teaching in this spirit. Given a mathematical system defined by various structural features, these colleagues ask their students to think away each of these features one by one and to explore the consequences of doing so, in imagination. The name Brown and Walter give their scheme serves as an apt emblem of the powers of negative thinking: they call it "What if Not?"[11]

III. Forgetting, or Lest We Remember

Forgetting is commonly considered an educational defect, memory a virtue. We rarely stop to think what a blessing forgetting is and how disabling memory can be. The late psychologist, A. R. Luria, has given us, in his book, *The Mind of a Mnemonist,* the case study of a man with enormous powers of memory, whose problem was the need to forget. "If," to take one example from Luria's account, "a passage were read to him quickly, one image would collide with another in his mind; images would begin to crowd in upon one another and would become contorted. How then was he to understand anything in this chaos of images?"[12] Remembering too much tended to extinguish the abstract significance of the passage.

Now this is of course a quite extreme case, but our ordinary experience yields a variety of examples where the elimination of traces rather than their preservation is what is required. Take first the learning of skills, e.g., skating, dancing, driving, swimming, typing, where the object is economy and grace of performance. Here suppression of our early halting steps is clearly functional; the traces of our stumblings, thrashings, and miscues are to be wiped out, the chisel marks smoothed away. If, as you type, you try to remember the clumsy movements of your fingers when you first learned, your present performance will be disrupted.

Even the initial rules for correct performance we may have been given are superseded and in time turn opaque. Max Black has described this process as one of "phenomenological compression" or "condensation" of the original formula. The experienced chess player, in his example, no longer uses the cumbersome rule he initially learned for the movement of the Knight. He

> comes to *see* the target square as available for the Knight ... and the criteria embodied in the original formula may be so effectively suppressed that "verbal articulation" may be disconcertingly difficult. [Such "intuitive transformation" of rules Black deems to be] of fundamental importance to educational method. ... Whatever the topic—a mathematical proof, the conjugation of a verb, the salient features of the Industrial Revolution— the data must be "rendered down," simplified, structured, if they are to be assimilated, remembered and properly used.[13]

Remembering these data under their new structure, it must be added, requires a progressive suppression of their initial structure. Remembering here builds on forgetting.

In areas of personal life, we often recognize the virtues of forgetting. To a friend who tends to preserve a memory of every slight or to cry over spilt milk, we may say "Forget it!"—thus acknowledging that memory is not always desirable. Yet in the realm of cognitive learning, we tend to overlook the parallel idea, that is, that some things deserve forgetting.

In these days of the so-called knowledge explosion, we have, it is true, been sensitized to the expansion of scholarly publication and the inevitable inability to take it all in. Luckily, to dignify each item published in the scholarly journals as "knowledge" is surely an exaggeration. Much, it is safe to say, is trivial, much is derivative, a good deal is worthless. Of what remains, only the tiniest fraction may bear on issues that concern a given learner, scholar, or professional. When we add to scholarly publication the torrent of words that bombards us from all sides in popular format, the situation becomes desperate.

Without the ability to ignore and forget, to turn a deaf ear to claims on our attention, we could develop no sustained cognitive efforts, no steady intellectual habits; constant distraction would be our lot. The urgent problem this situation presents to us is how to develop criteria for filtering the significant from the trivial, how to decide what to read and what to pass by, what to learn and what to ignore, what to remember and what to forget. This is at once a practical, an intellectual, and a moral problem that ought to be faced and dealt with in education. And it is a problem that cannot readily be raised unless we recognize that to be forgotten is the proper fate of much that is communicated to us. To recognize the problem would, in any case, go far in mitigating the emphasis on examinations based on memory, which still reigns over so much of education's dominion.

Here again, William James is a sure guide when he writes:

> We are all too apt to measure the gains of our pupils by their proficiency in directly reproducing in a recitation or an examination such matters as they may have learned, and inarticulate power in them is something of which we always underestimate the value. . . . But this is a great mistake. It is but a small part of our experience in life that we are ever able articulately to recall. And yet the whole of it has had its influence in shaping our character and defining our tendencies to judge and act. Although the ready memory is a great blessing to its possessor, the vaguer memory of a subject, of having once had to do with it, of its neighborhood, and of where we may go to recover it again, constitutes in most men and women the chief fruit of their education. This is true even in professional education. The doctor, the lawyer, are seldom able to decide upon a case off-hand. They differ from other men only through the fact that they know how to get at the materials for decision in five minutes or half an hour: whereas the layman is unable to get at the materials at all. . . .
> Be patient, then, and sympathetic with the type of mind that cuts a poor

figure in examinations. It may, in the long examination which life sets us, come out in the end in better shape than the glib and ready reproducer, its passions being deeper, its purposes more worthy, its combining power less commonplace, and its total mental output consequently more important.[14]

IV. Guesswork, or I Guess So

Guessing has long been deemed an academic defect. The pupil is supposed to know the right answer and not to guess at it. "Either you know it or you don't" is the attitude of innumerable teachers, parents and test-makers, past and present, but it is no more realistic for being so widely shared. The fact is that the capacity for guessing is one of the most important—perhaps *the* most important—mental capacity we have, without which we would be so handicapped as not to be able to sustain our very lives.

In one of its senses guessing may be identified with estimation of some numerical value; in another and broader sense, it may be equated with theorizing. Both senses have in common that the guess goes beyond what is known or can be ascertained for sure. Take first estimation. You want to know the number of cookies in the jar but have no time to count them; you want to know the length of the bookshelf but cannot actually measure it; you want to decide how much money to take along on your trip in order to cover expenses. In no case do you have an answer that is certainly right, but that does not mean that every answer is equally wrong. There are better and worse ways to deal with such problems of estimation even if, in the nature of the case, they work by indirection and yield approximations ruled by probability. Probability is after all, as Bishop Butler said, the very guide of life.[15]

Now consider explanatory or predictive theories rather than numerical estimates. Our theories as to why things happen and what may be expected to happen set the context for all of life's activities. Not one step do we take, not one decision do we make that does not depend on such theories, yet their status is commonly misconceived. They are thought, in the case of science at least, to rest on a solid basis of fact. Some textbooks even speak of "theory construction" as if theories were systematically built on a firm foundation of factual evidence.

But there simply is no systematic method for constructing theories. They are not in fact built but guessed. Science can indeed be described, in Michael Polanyi's words, as "a consistent effort at guessing" and "the propositions of science" as "in the nature of guesses."[16] Evidence, to be sure, plays a critical role in the testing of scientific theories, but no theory can be tested that is not first formulated. That initial formulation goes well beyond all accumulated evidence. It is neither self-evident nor logically derived from the facts we have. Guesswork is its true source; its only method is what

Einstein described as "a free play with concepts."[17] Not the eradication but the cultivation of guessing is the proper goal of education—guessing that is not simply the flipping of a coin but is responsive to the problem at hand and committed to the verdicts of ongoing tests. To build such guesswork into the educational experience of our students is a primary challenge to educators.

V. Irrelevance, or What's the Point

That everything educational has a point is a popular dogma. In America, this is often interpreted as saying that every subject of the curriculum has to justify itself by its usefulness; each unit of teaching needs to be shown relevant to the future life of the student or of the nation if it is to be allowed a place in schooling. Everything in education is thus thrown on the defensive; it is guilty until proven innocent.

The effect is that some subjects are scanted or demoted in significance; others are simply distorted. Thus, the arts are conceived as mere frill; history, in Henry Ford's immortal phrase, "is bunk";[18] ethics is a luxury or an intrusion, while mathematics and the sciences are taught with primary emphasis on their technological applications. All of education becomes a handmaiden of utility, which rules the system.

But why is utility given such preeminent status? Is it obvious that everything has a point? What is the point of Beethoven's Rasoumovsky Quartets, of what use is the Mona Lisa, what is the usefulness of Fermat's Last Theorem, Aristotle's physics, Kant's *Groundwork of the Metaphysic of Morals,* Plato's *Republic,* of Chaucer's *Canterbury Tales?* If having a point is so interpreted as to declare these works pointless, the dogma of relevance loses all credibility. On the other hand, if they are conceded to *have point,* that is to say, significance, independently of having *a* point, that is, some useful application, the idea of excluding or demoting them in schooling is robbed of its force.

Such works do not gain their significance as means to the achievement of certain ends independently defined. Rather, they help to define the ends that confer significance on other things as means. Holding exemplars of value before the growing mind is justification enough for various elements of education. For the job of education is not only to provide persons with useful techniques but also to provide techniques with persons who have been made sensitive to the endless quest for knowledge and ideal values. If the fruit of schooling is its use in life, it must indeed be a life itself infused with a respect for knowledge and value.[19]

VI. Procrastination, or Don't Do it Now

Can anything good be said about procrastination, that favorite whipping boy of parents, educators, and efficiency experts? Yes, a good deal, upon reflection. In any sensible ordering of one's affairs, some things need putting off. I refer not merely to the psychologists' concept of delayed gratification, the capacity for which is thought to be a sign of maturity, but also, first of all, to delayed worry, the capacity for which is a boon to mental health. When multiple cares crowd in upon a person, often in the dead of a sleepless night but frequently as well in the heat of the day, the ability to sort these cares by temporal urgency is of enormous benefit. What I have in mind here is the ability to distribute one's several worries along a time line running into the indefinite future, thus relieving their combined pressure upon the present and allowing them to be dealt with one by one. Scarlett O'Hara's "I'll think about that tomorrow" is often a good policy.

Second, there is the putting off of various tasks and duties in the interests primarily of efficiency rather than emotional relief. Rational planning will normally require postponement of some tasks in favor of others to prevent gridlock and consequent paralysis of effort. Of course, important tasks undone may generate their own worries, so the concerns of planning merge with those of mental health. A psychiatrist friend once gave me his criterion for a good administrator, namely, the ability to tolerate a cluttered desk. His point, I take it, was that the urge to keep one's desk clean is likely to produce both inefficiency and mental stress.

Finally, there are certain tasks that themselves require a separation of phases. Writing is a prime example of such a task, where the first draft needs to be differentiated from the consequent editing phase. To collapse these two phases into one is a formula for paralysis. Some advisees of mine have begun work on their dissertations by attempting to frame a perfect first sentence. Finding this effort impossibly daunting, they have seen the completed dissertation receding more and more into the future, ever further away and beyond all hope of attainment. I have urged these advisees to put off editing until they had a sizeable chunk to edit, asking them what they would think of a sculptor who attempted to create a human figure by first sculpting a perfect thumb. I wanted these students to procrastinate, to delay editing to a later time.

Even in creating a first draft, a writer needs to cut a large job into smaller bits, lest the conception of the whole intimidate him into silence. A student who says "Today I'm writing my dissertation" may find the day's task magnified beyond all feasible successful effort, whereas to say "Today I'm writing Section One of Chapter 1" marks out a do-able job and liberates the writer from everything else. Procrastination here pays off.

A striking image, for me, of the two-phase task is the landing of a spaceship on the moon. About sixteen years ago, Professor Joseph Weizenbaum of M.I.T., in a conversation with several friends at the Stanford Center, challenged us laymen to explain the remarkable fact that a rocket aimed at an object so far away could reach the target with unerring accuracy. He himself provided the answer. The initial shot required no pinpoint accuracy; it needed only to bring the spaceship into the general area of the moon, whereupon the ship's own guidance system could take over the residual task of putting the vehicle down. Procrastination respecting the actual landing made the whole task possible to execute.

VII. Idleness, or Let The World Go By

Idleness is surely the bane of American educators. Effort, diligence, activity—that's the ticket. From the behaviorist's industrial efficiency model of schooling through the progressives' learning by doing doctrine to today's emphasis on "time-on-task," we have exalted the virtues of work, work, work, in education. It is perhaps especially because American educational *practice* has been so relaxed, when compared to the practices of countries with more selective systems, that the emphasis on work has figured so strongly in American educational *theory*.

Now work is certainly a good thing, provided it is substantive and not mere busy work, provided intellectual advance is not confused with overt physical movements or mechanical drill or the shuffling of papers hither and yon. But true intellectual advance is hard to track, it cannot be coerced or imposed as a duty, satisfying neither the moral puritan nor the efficiency expert with time clock at the ready. For it is often withdrawn and private, looking suspiciously like daydreaming. The silent pupil with the faraway look in his or her eyes may in fact be the one making the strongest mental gains.

Such a pupil was Albert Einstein, whose "aversion to the constant drill" in his gymnasium led to his being asked to leave the school. He had from early childhood "been inclined," in the words of one of his biographers, "to separate himself from children of his own age and to engage in daydreaming and meditative musing."[20] Of course, the young Albert was not your average student. But neither is it the case that only rare intellectual geniuses grow through exercise of the imagination. And it must, in any event, give one pause to consider Einstein's mature criticism of what he calls coercive methods of education, requiring drill and cramming for set examinations. He writes:

> It is, in fact, nothing short of a miracle that the modern methods of instruction have not yet entirely strangled the holy curiosity of inquiry; for this delicate little plant, aside from stimulation, stands mainly in need of freedom; without this it goes to wreck and ruin without fail. It is a very grave mistake to think that the enjoyment of seeing and searching can be promoted by means of coercion and a sense of duty. To the contrary, I believe that it would be possible to rob even a healthy beast of prey of its voraciousness, if it were feasible, with the aid of a whip, to force the beast

to devour continuously, even when not hungry, especially if the food, handed out under such coercion, were to be selected accordingly.[21]

Daydreaming may seem idle to the educational moralist—not work but mere play. We have then to remind the moralist that this form of play is often serious business and needs recognition and appreciation. In the words of John Dewey, the "supreme mark and criterion of a teacher" is the ability to bypass externals and to "keep track of [the child's] mental play, to recognize the signs of its presence or absence, to know how it is initiated and maintained, how to test it by results attained, and to test *apparent* results by it."[22]

Students of thinking tell us, further, that even real dreams may do intellectual work, and the history of science provides ample evidence. A striking case is Kekulé's discovery of the ring structure of the benzene molecule, after dozing in front of the fire and dreaming of snakes dancing in ring-like formations.[23] The notion of the incubation of a problem, where, without conscious attention to it, the mind silently works out a solution, has been long known and credited in experience. Sometimes the best approach to a problem is to turn away from it completely, let the mental machinery idle, go for a walk, take in a movie, have a cup of cocoa.

To acknowledge the role of what I have called "idleness" in education is to strive not only to address the pupil's mind and will, but also to capture his dreams, not only to assign him work, but also to promote his play and to appreciate his spontaneity. This is a hard thing for teachers to do when they themselves are often viewed as minor technicians within a bureaucratic process, burdened by stringent social demands while their own spontaneity and initiative are unappreciated.[24] The issue therefore has to do ultimately not just with teachers but, as William James recognized in his essay "The Gospel of Relaxation," with all of us who form the community within which education is carried on. His message is quite general:

Unclamp . . . your intellectual and practical machinery, and let it run free.[25]

Conclusion

I have now ended my argument. I trust you will not misunderstand me to be urging that our schools set about producing contrary, forgetful, idling ignoramuses, devoid of a proper sense of relevance and forever putting off until tomorrow what needs doing today. Rather, I have tried to rescue several virtues hidden in what are presently seen as unredeemable vices. Recognizing these virtues underneath their disguises can only serve, I am convinced, to enhance the processes by which we educate our children.

Notes

1. William James, *Talks To Teachers on Psychology: And to Students on Some of Life's Ideals* (New York: Norton, 1958), pp. 49–51.

2. Ibid., pp. 51–52.

3. Ibid., p. 52.

4. Ibid., pp. 52–53.

5. John Stuart Mill, "On Genius," selections from which are included, along with interpretive discussion, in Kingsley Price, *Education and Philosophical Thought* (Boston: Allyn & Bacon, 1962), chap. 9.

6. Some criticisms of educational uses of the computer and allied notions of information are contained in my "Computers at School?" *Teachers College Record* 87, no. 4 (Summer 1986): 513–28. See Chapter 8 above.

7. See my *Reason and Teaching* (Indianapolis, Ind.: Hackett, 1973), p. 71, and related discussion in my *Conditions of Knowledge* (Chicago: University of Chicago Press, 1965), chap. 3.

8. Michael Oakeshott, "Learning and Teaching," in *The Concept of Education* ed. R. S. Peters (London: Routledge & Kegan Paul, 1967), p. 162.

9. Michael Oakeshott, "Political Education," in his *Rationalism in Politics* (New York: Basic Books, 1962); reprinted in I. Scheffler, *Philosophy and Education*, 2d ed. (Boston: Allyn & Bacon, 1966), p. 344. The passage quoted refers specifically to political education, but can, I believe, be taken more generally, as I have done here.

10. Karl Popper, *The Logic of Scientific Discovery* (London: Hutchinson, 1959).

11. Marion Walter and Stephen Brown, "What-If-Not," *Mathematics Teaching*, no. 46 (Spring 1969); 38–45. See also their *The Art of Problem Posing* (Philadelphia: The Franklin Institute Press, 1983).

12. A. R. Luria, *The Mind of a Mnemonist* (Cambridge, Mass.: Harvard University Press, 1987), p. 112.

13. Max Black, "Rules and Routines," in R. S. Peters, ed. *The Concept of Education*, pp. 100–101.

14. William James, *Talks to Teachers*, pp. 100–101.

15. Joseph Butler, D.C. L., *The Works of Bishop Butler*, vol. 2: *The Analogy of Religion: Natural and Revealed* (London: Macmillan, 1900), "Introduction," p. 2.

16. M. Polanyi, *Science, Faith, and Society* (Chicago: University of Chicago Press, 1964), pp. 23 and 31.

17. Albert Einstein, "Autobiographial Notes," trans. P. A. Schilpp, in *Albert Einstein: Philosopher-Scientist*, ed. P. A. Schilpp (New York: Tudor, 1949), p. 13.

18. See Keith Sward, *The Legend of Henry Ford* (New York: Rinehart, 1948), p. 110.

19. See my *Reason and Teaching*, p. 135.

20. Philipp Frank, *Einstein: His Life and Times* (New York: Alfred A. Knopf, 1947), pp. 8, 10, and 17.

21. Albert Einstein, "Autobiographical Notes," pp. 17 and 19.

22. John Dewey, "The Relation of Theory to Practice in Education," in *The Relation of Theory to Practice in the Education of Teachers*, 3d Yearbook, 1, of the National Society for The Scientific Study of Education (Bloomington, Illinois: Public School Publishing,

1904); reprinted in Merle L. Borrowman, *Teacher Education in America: A Documentary History* (New York: Columbia Teachers College Press, 1965).

23. See, for a brief account, C. G. Hempel, *Philosophy of National Science* (Englewood Cliffs, N.J.: Prentice Hall, 1966), p. 16., p. 16 fn. 7.

24. See my *Reason and Teaching,* p. 61.

25. William James, *Talks to Teachers,* p. 144.

Part V

Pragmatic Perspectives

13

John Dewey's Social and Educational Theory

The key to Dewey's social and educational theory is his emphasis on wholeness. He urges an increasing awareness of the infinite context of our action, a continual growth in meaning through an expansion of intelligent activity. Thus he views education as continuous growth. Thus he judges social and political institutions by their capacity to enable individual persons to develop in power and awareness. Thus he demands of schools that they present the studies in relation to one another and link available knowledge with the live context beyond the classroom.

Dewey is not a religious thinker, but in *Human Nature and Conduct* he offers an interpretation of the theme of wholeness in religious terms:

> Infinite relationships of man with his fellows and with nature already exist. The ideal means, as we have seen, a sense of these encompassing continuities with their infinite reach. This meaning even now attaches to present activities because they are set in a whole to which they belong and which belongs to them. Even in the midst of conflict, struggle and defeat a consciousness is possible of the enduring and comprehending whole.[1]

Such a consciousness requires symbols, but the symbols of the past no longer serve.[2] "Religion has lost itself in cults, dogmas, and myths":

> Religion as a sense of the whole is the most individualized of all things, the most spontaneous, undefinable and varied. For individuality signifies unique connections in the whole. Yet it has been perverted into something uniform and immutable. . . . Instead of marking the freedom and peace of the individual as a member of an infinite whole, it has been petrified into a slavery of thought and sentiment, an intolerant superiority on the part of the few and an intolerable burden on the part of the many.[3]

This selection is from my *Four Pragmatists* (London: Routledge & Kegan Paul, 1974), pp. 240–55.

Although he is critical of actual religions, Dewey identifies the religious sense as a sense of the whole, and holds that "every act may carry within itself a consoling and supporting consciousness of the whole to which it belongs and which in some sense belongs to it."[4] In a vein reminiscent of James's discussion of the moral holidays afforded by belief in the Absolute, Dewey suggests that a consciousness of the whole allows an emancipation from its burdens, which is yet consistent with responsible action:

> There is a conceit fostered by perversion of religion which assimilates the universe to our personal desires; but there is also a conceit of carrying the load of the universe from which religion liberates us. Within the flickering inconsequential acts of separate selves dwells a sense of the whole which claims and dignifies them. In its presence we put off morality and live in the universal. The life of the community in which we live and have our being is the fit symbol of this relationship. The acts in which we express our perception of the ties which bind us to others are its only rites and ceremonies.[5]

The community is, thus, a symbol of the whole, consciousness of which offers the only religious consolation Dewey acknowledges as significant. The whole is, however, infinite and so cannot be grasped as complete. We may approximate it in our experience through the conception of growth, growth without end—in awareness, sensitivity, and meaning. The community ideally fit to symbolize the whole is one that frees itself and its members to grow.

An ideal society, for Dewey, is an association that allows for maximum growth of each person, through his own activity and self-development. Such an association aims to institutionalize intelligence in matters of conduct, as natural science institutionalizes intelligence in investigations of nature. It is free of artificial barriers dividing its members from one another, it fosters the free exchange of ideas, and it treats the ideas underlying its common activities as hypotheses—open to the test of experience, criticizable by all whom such activities affect, and revisable by procedures enlisting their common consent.

This is the ideal of democracy. The machinery of democracy is not an end in itself but a means directed toward such an ideal. The justification of democracy is not to be sought in some mythical infallibility of democratic procedures. Rather it is to be sought in the *quality* of human action promoted by institutions that acknowledge each person's dignity and judgment in forms of public exchange and participation in the public life.

> The keynote of democracy as a way of life may be expressed, it seems to me, as the necessity for the participation of every mature human being in formation of the values that regulate the living of men together: which is

necessary from the standpoint of both the general social welfare and the full development of human beings as individuals.[6]

Democratic political forms are means to an end. They rest

> upon the idea that no man or limited set of men is wise enough or good enough to rule others without their consent; the positive meaning of this statement is that all those who are affected by social institutions must have a share in producing and managing them. The two facts that each one is influenced in what he does and enjoys and in what he becomes by the institutions under which he lives, and that therefore he shall have, in a democracy, a voice in shaping them, are the passive and active sides of the same fact.[7]

When social institutions exclude certain persons from the development of their own powers, it is not only they as individuals who suffer, but also "the whole social body" that is deprived of their intelligence, judgment, and contribution. And there is one thing in particular that excluded persons are "wiser about than anybody else can be, and that is where the shoe pinches, the troubles they suffer from."[8] Authoritarian schemes assume that the value of a person's contribution may be judged

> by some *prior* principle, if not of family and birth or race and color or possession of material wealth, then by the position and rank a person occupies in the existing social scheme. The democratic faith in equality is the faith that each individual shall have the chance and opportunity to contribute whatever he is capable of contributing and that the value of his contribution be decided by its place and function in the organized total of similar contributions, not on the basis of prior status of any kind whatever.[9]

Of all the freedoms required by the democratic outlook, freedom of *mind* is basic, for without it, individuals are not genuinely free to develop. "Freed intelligence . . . is necessary to direct and to warrant freedom of action."[10] Cultivation of intelligence under conditions of freedom is thus at once, for Dewey, the fundamental imperative of democracy and the main task of education.

Institutionally, education may, in fact, be viewed as the formal agency for fostering intelligence. Its primary aim is to develop the habits and mentality of critical thinking in application to all spheres of life. As an institution, it may itself be operated more or less intelligently. For it to be run intelligently, it should incorporate the general values of the democratic ideal, and its procedures should be developed and reviewed in a critical and scientific manner. This implies, fundamentally, that educational policy is to be stated and criticized in the public forum and that all concerned in education ought to be heard. It implies also that educational procedures are to be judged by their fruits rather than their origins; curriculum and teaching methods, school organization and grouping, grading and testing—all are open to critical review in the light of empirical consequences scientifically assessed. It emphatically does not follow from Dewey's view that the educational past is to be rejected in a wholesale manner. On the contrary, the funded wisdom of the past provides a valuable guide to present activity. But guiding ideas are not dogmas; they are tested by the very activities they help to organize. They must continue to prove themselves by their consequences. If we are alert to this fact, we will profit from their guidance and we will also learn from critical experience how to improve upon them.

The aim of education, according to Dewey, is first and foremost to develop critical methods of thought. Its task is not to indoctrinate a particular point of view but rather to help generate those powers of assessment and criticism by which diverse points of view may themselves be responsibly judged. In pursuit of this task, the school ought to *exemplify* the application of critical method to all the domains of human life. This implies the need to present these domains with an emphasis upon their *meaning*, that is, in their relatedness to one another but, most particularly, in their bearing upon the realm of purposive activity. For the more meaning we grasp, the greater the context we can take into account and the more we are able to evaluate critically. This is the central idea of Dewey's theory of education, which he develops into a notion of proper method and curriculum:

> Study is effectual in the degree in which the pupil realizes the place of the
> . . . truth he is dealing with in carrying to fruition activities in which he is
> concerned. This connection of an object and a topic with the promotion
> of an activity having a purpose is the first and the last word of a genuine
> theory of interest in education.[11]

Proper method requires that the subject be placed in a broad, and growing, context— a context that embraces the student's own purposes and potential activities as well as the urgent problems confronting the human community of which he is a part.

In the matter of curriculum, Dewey's emphasis is on continuity and meaning. Selection and specialization are, of course, necessary in modern schooling, but we must take care not to erect practical separations into hard and fast divisions among the studies. For every such division disrupts an array of real connections and so impoverishes the meaning of the subjects taught:

> The subject matter of education consists primarily of the meanings which
> supply content to existing social life. The continuity of social life means
> that many of these meanings are contributed to present activity by past

collective experience. As social life grows more complex, these factors increase in number and import. There is need of special selection, formulation, and organization in order that they may be adequately transmitted to the new generation. But this very process tends to set up subject matter as something of value just by itself, apart from its function in promoting the realization of the meanings implied in the present experience of the immature.[12]

Divisions between higher and lower studies, between theoretical and applied, between scientific and humanistic, between literary and technological studies—all are devices of convenience at best. Taken in any more serious fashion, they are all mischievous. We may need to use them, but we need also to help the student to see through them. For the full meaning of technology cannot be appreciated unless it is put into connection with its theoretical base and its human import; humanistic studies are, likewise, impoverished if they are isolated from contact with the social world and the science that is transforming it. A fundamental continuity of intimation, development, and human significance, moreover, unites studies that are elementary and advanced, basic and applied.

Integration of the curriculum is primarily a matter of recognizing that "all studies grow out of relations in the one great common world."[13] Studies are to be interrelated as varied avenues of access to this world and as valuable resources for the solution of common problems. In *Democracy and Education* Dewey argues that the school is not simply a mirror image of society; it represents a simplified, idealized, and balanced environment with its own long-range goals of cultivating intelligent habits of mind.[14] Yet the impact of such cultivation is ultimately social, and the process of cultivation of such habits is one that requires genuine reference to environing social conditions within which the school has its being and role. It is this long-range social role that provides integration and coherence to the varied specialized activities of schooling.

Dewey envisages a society that allows the maximum growth of each person through an expansion of his own capabilities for intelligent and effective action. Such a society, although it is based on the concept of indefinite and varied growth in its individual members, is far from indefinite and indeterminate itself. It requires institutions that foster free expression of ideas, toleration of diversity, and the participation of its members in "formation of the values that regulate the living of men together."[15] Moreover, such institutions themselves require supporting habits of mind, in particular, habits that are consonant with critical and scientific thought. Dewey has been criticized for taking growth as his basic value, without specifying the direction or ultimate goal of growth. But, as he might reply, the outcomes of growth cannot thus be restricted without substituting an uncritical constraint in advance for the operation of intelligence, thereby placing an unwarranted limitation upon the freedom of activity. Furthermore, as we have seen, the ideals of intelligence, growth, and freedom, open-ended as they are, are not amorphous or directionless; indeed, they make the most stringent of demands upon those who would embody them in human institutions and strive to rear their young by their light.

The schooling Dewey advocates is analogous in its rationale. It is designed to cultivate critical habits of mind. This aim, according to Dewey's general analysis of thought, requires the involvement of the pupil's own purposes in the learning process and the relating of the school's studies to problems of the environing society. But schooling, in Dewey's scheme, is not therefore amorphous or undemanding. It is organized around problems, and it is directed toward internalizing in the pupil the discipline of critical and responsible thinking.

Dewey's educational views have been subjected to contrary criticisms. On the one hand, he has been charged with counseling extreme permissiveness—a kind of anarchy in the classroom. On the other hand, he has been accused of exalting the social role of the school to the detriment of individuality—urging a society of conformists. He has been held to be radically disruptive of the ordered ways and traditions of the past and also to be a conservative, urging inculcation of an inflexible belief in the values of the surrounding society.

These opposed forms of criticism cannot be simultaneously held, for they cancel one another. Moreover, each overshoots the mark, exaggerating some element of Dewey's thought to the point of distortion and ignoring the fundamental allegiance to critical, experimental thought that lends balance to his educational doctrines.

Dewey wants to enlist the student's purposes in learning, so that the relation of the various studies to his own choices may become evident. Such a procedure requires a problem-organization of materials; it is calculated to enhance the meaning of the studies while increasing the student's sense of effectiveness as a purposive and intelligent agent. It is a crude mistake to take Dewey as advocating activity for its own sake. The whole point of activity in his scheme is that it should, so far as possible, be made educative through the guiding power of ideas and the critical assessment of consequences. This undertaking may be very difficult to execute, or otherwise inadequate; it surely cannot be characterized as simply permissive. Not only does it retain the materials of adult studies under a new educational organization, but it imposes the structure inherent in definite purposes, requiring special instrumentalities for their realization. Dewey is not opposed to discipline; he wants the school, so far as possible, to strive for an internalization of intellectual discipline rather than construing discipline as primarily a matter of enforcement from without. As with scientific research or the practice of the arts, crafts and professions, discipline ought, he believes, to grow from the first-hand struggle to solve specific problems, from encountering the resistance of available resources, experimenting with alternative ideas, putting them to the hard test of experience, evaluating them in the light of guiding purposes. To acquire the discipline born of struggle with problems is to incorporate habits of critical method; such incorporation is not a *laissez faire* or easy task—it both enlists and helps to foster dedicated effort, care, responsibility, and self-control. It is this conception of discipline as growing out of purposive problem-solving activity that ought, in Dewey's view, to predominate in education.

Nor is Dewey eager to foster a society of conformists, as should be evident from even a cursory reading of his work. Certainly, he wants the work of the school to be related to basic problems of the environing society. In this way, he believes, the meaning of schoolwork may be enlarged and the effectiveness of knowledge made increasingly apparent; at the same time, the urgent difficulties of the common life may be illuminated and the moral habit of coping reliably with them may be encouraged in the young. To take social problems as a significant focus for schooling is, however, by no means to advocate inculcation of a social dogma. Dewey explicitly warns against social indoctrination; the fundamental allegiance of the school ought to be an allegiance to critical methods of analysis. Such methods are inimical to conformity: they demand responsible and independent judgment of social issues by canons of scientific reasoning and assessment of data.

Dewey emphasizes the social climate of the school, to be sure. His point, however, is not to foster conformity but to alert teachers to the learning that goes on outside the formal lessons of the classroom. Insofar as critical habits of mind and character are related to the human arrangements within which academic lessons are set, teachers need to be aware of the influence of such arrangements and to take responsibility for the moral and intellectual habits they foster. These habits ought, ideally, to be consonant with scientific and responsible thought, they ought to foster the independence of mind, the respect for others, and the capability of adjudicating differences by orderly methods that are characteristic both of democratic and of scientific attitudes. Allegiance to method rather than conformity to creed is the keynote.

Dewey's educational vision is designed neither to uphold the past, as such, nor to disrupt it, as such. Continuity with the past is, in any case, inevitable, as are departures from it, in one or another respect. The point is to strive to develop habits of intelligence that may be applied to life's problems. The deliverances of intelligent analysis may, in certain cases, counsel revision or rejection of inherited ways; in other cases, they may counsel retention. The widespread development of intelligent and responsible habits of mind would, however, in itself, constitute a large change in society, capable of bringing critical evaluation to bear on the problems and practices of our common life. It is this long-range development of intelligent habits of mind that is the school's role, in Dewey's view. To succeed in this development, the school must take society's problems seriously, but this by no means requires it to stamp prevalent social values into the minds of its children. The school must also strive to deepen reflection, strengthen independence, and develop critical skills in application to social issues, to a degree that has not yet been achieved. But this is by no means tantamount to counseling a wholesale disruption of the past. It is, rather, to conceive the school's task as enabling society to cope with its problems more intelligently, more effectively, more imaginatively, and more responsibly than it has so far done.

I should, myself, however, wish to offer certain criticisms of Dewey's views, despite my agreement with much of what he has to say on educational matters. Since I have elsewhere elaborated some of these criticisms[16] I will here note them only briefly.

First, I suggest that the notion of continuity is exaggerated in Dewey's treatment. Continuities are certainly important in education, and Dewey's emphasis on bringing together the humanistic and the technical, the elementary and the advanced, the disciplinary and the problematic elements of the educational process is a salutary one. He is, I believe, certainly right in attacking the idea that the studies are independent and external entities, self-enclosed and somehow rooted in nature. He is right in advocating that technical matters be illuminated by theoretical knowledge and seen from the perspective of their human significance. He is right, too, in demanding that an appreciation of values be supplemented by a realistic understanding of their natural conditions and vicissitudes. Nevertheless, discontinuities and distinctions are as natural as continuities, and they need also to be acknowledged where they exist.

Theory is, for example, surely connected with observation and with practice, but it is also autonomous; it has its own career and life. The general tendency of pragmatism is to interpret theory as intermediary between practical problem and practical resolution, and to construe its content wholly in terms of observable transformations of the world through practical effort. This characterization of theory does not seem to me tenable. Neither the content nor the function of theory can be fully understood by reference to the resolution of practical problems through transformations of the world. One must, to appreciate the force of a theory, grasp more than just its practical ramifications; theories serve not simply to guide practice, but also to afford us an intelligible and coherent representation of fundamental natural processes.

The process of theorizing is a creative process. It is not just a matter of cataloguing the functional relations among phenomenal changes, nor is it, in any plausible sense, generated out of experience. The theorist is free to invent, simplify, postulate, categorize, extrapolate, idealize—he may need to back away from the detail of phenomenal change and practical urgency in order to strive to "see through" to underlying elements and patterns. Distance, in other words, is functional for the theorist, who strives for ever deeper insights and broader perspectives on nature. The value of theoretical distance must be acknowledged in education and distinguished from mere remoteness and pedantry. In opposing the latter, we must avoid destruction of the former. Education ought, indeed, to encourage the theoretical motive, which, whether or not it promises to relate to practical solutions of social problems, aims to achieve a penetrating vision of natural structures.

Second, the problem-theory of thinking, as developed by Peirce and Dewey, seems to me inadequate. Problems cannot be identified with difficulties of practice; the problems that organize scientific research arise in a context of prior theory and experimentation. Moreover, the life of science is not exhausted in resolving problems that arise without effort; the scientist's thought does not subside when his questions have been answered. Problem-finding is as important as problem-solving, and scientific thought of the greatest significance is expended in seeking, formulating, and elaborating questions that have not yet intruded on practice.

We may note the difficulties in Peirce's conception of real doubt as the origin of inquiry, and his own recognition of the importance of feigned, hypothetical, and speculative questions.[17] We may also note the shortcomings of the problem-theory of reflection as support for Dewey's notion of continuous reconstruction and critical testing of ideas in action.[18] If we reflect upon the import of these criticisms for education, we should need to acknowledge both the possibility and the importance of encouraging the pupil to seek problems, of helping him to a wider perception and a richer sensitivity, a more insistent curiosity and a more active imagination. We should continue to value problem-solving as a method of educational organization, but we should place it within the context of a growing awareness that reaches out steadily to problems unperceived before.

The problem-theory of thinking seems to me also difficult in attempting to give a uniform analysis of thought in all realms. I have argued that it does not even give an adequate picture of scientific thought, the preferred domain of pragmatic interpretations. Much less does it provide an analysis that can smoothly contain not only the scientific imagination but also the work of the artist, the historian, the poet, the translator, the inventor, the novelist, the mathematician. Much of our thinking is problem-oriented, but much is not: much grows out of free speculation, playfulness, curiosity, or out of the need to express, describe, or create. One can attempt to force all these varieties into a common abstract framework, but the advantages of doing so would need to be so evident as to override the cost in artificiality and generality. I do not think the problem-theory is adequate in this respect; even if it were, we should need to provide, in education, a concrete and realistic awareness of the special features differentiating science from history, art from mathematics, poetry from legal reasoning, philology from philosophy. We should, in other words, need to transmit the several traditions of thought as we now possess them, rather than simply filtering them through an abstract philosophical schema of thinking as problem-solving.

Third, while I applaud Dewey's emphasis on meaning in his account of education, I suggest that it is of variable relevance in the educational process. That is to say, the meaning of subjects is indeed enhanced through their mutual connectedness as well as through their incorporation into the student's context of purpose and potential action. Moreover, the teacher himself ought to have as clear a conception as possible of the aims, values, and criteria that animate his educational choices of curriculum as well as methods and organization. Nevertheless, learning does not need to proceed, at every point, through linkages to prior purpose; the pupil does not, I suggest, need to learn everything in the context of its meanings and uses. Children learn many things as they do language, or games—through participation, curiosity, or the sheer joy of the activity. The teacher ought to be clear as to the meaning and value of introducing a particular subject or educational activity and enlisting participation as if it were a game. But the child may well learn it, efficiently and joyfully, as a game. It is, in principle, an empirical question whether mathematics is better taught through elaborate reference to the meaning of fundamental concepts and operations than through intuitive and gamelike methods. This question ought, at any rate, not be begged by a philosophical predilection for meaning in education.

What is certainly of basic importance is that, no matter how a child has been introduced to a subject, his capacity for meaningful action, intelligent criticism, and growth in understanding should not be destroyed or stunted through his education. Whatever hospitals do, as Florence Nightingale is reputed to have said, they at least ought not to spread disease. No matter what schools do, they should not cripple educational growth. The child's questions, his attempts to understand, should always be respected and sincerely met. His efforts to criticize, to relate, to utilize, and to elaborate ought always to be strengthened and encouraged, so that he becomes ever more aware of his intellectual agency, its powers and responsibilities. This does not imply, however, that he needs to have all things explained to him before questions arise, that he is incapable of stepping out of the familiar circle of his projects and purposes to explore the world beyond without prior assurances of meaning.

Finally, I believe that Dewey's view of the school underestimates its autonomy, for it emphasizes as the primary role of the school its long-range transformation of society through its ultimate impact on problems of the larger culture. Dewey's view of the school is by no means a simple-minded one; he does not see the school as a mere reflection of society, nor does he suppose it to be an instrument for accomplishing social purposes set in advance. The social end that is served by the school is represented, for him, not by society as it happens to be but by a reformed society, illuminated by critical intelligence. Nevertheless, he emphasizes the intermediary role of the school, as an agency capable of transforming problematic conditions, through the cultivation of intelligence, into more harmonious and satisfactory arrangements. To this end, he stresses the continuity between school and society, placing social problems at the center of the school's focus.

As is already apparent from my earlier remarks on the autonomy of theory, I believe the work of the school is not adequately represented by Dewey's account. In fostering theory, the school ought, in a basic sense, to stand apart from life, not by propagating pedantry and myth, but by encouraging the theoretical illumination of a world that is wider than the school and wider even than the society in which the school is placed. The school requires sufficient distance from society to enable it to develop intellectual concerns and cultural standards that have their own worth, quite apart from the resolution of social problems, and that may, moreover, place those very problems in a new perspective. The school may be viewed as an intermediary agency helping to improve society in the long run, but society may equally be viewed as an intermediary agency to be judged by its dedication to the autonomous values of intelligence, criticism, knowledge, and art, of which the school is the guardian. The school, in my view, ought to see itself *not simply* as instrumental to an improved society, although it ought to see itself in that way, surely. Its job is not only to serve but also to enlighten, create, understand, and illuminate, efforts that have intrinsic value and dignity, efforts that are themselves to be served by the society of men and women.

Notes

1. John Dewey, *Human Nature and Conduct* (New York: Henry Holt, 1922, 1930), p. 330.

2. Ibid.,

3. Ibid., p. 331.

4. Ibid.

5. Ibid., pp. 331–32.

6. John Dewey, "Democracy and Educational Administration" (an address to the National Education Association, 1937), *School and Society* 45 (3 April 1937): 457–62. Cited passage reprinted in *Intelligence in the Modern World: John Dewey's Philosophy,* ed. Joseph Ratner (New York: Modern Library, 1939), p. 400.

7. Ibid., p. 401.

8. Ibid., p. 402.

9. Ibid., pp. 403–4.

10. Ibid., p. 404.

11. John Dewey, *Democracy and Education* (New York: Macmillan, [original date 1916] 1961), p. 135.

12. Ibid., p. 192.

13. John Dewey, *The School and Society* (Chicago: University of Chicago Press, 1899), p. 103.

14. See Dewey, *Democracy and Education*, pp. 20–22.

15. Dewey, in Ratner, ed., *Intelligence in the Modern World: John Dewey's Philosophy* (New York: Modern Library, 1939), p. 400.

16. I. Scheffler, "Educational Liberalism and Dewey's Philosophy," *Harvard Educational Review* 26 (1956): 190–98; and I. Scheffler, "Reflections on Educational Relevance," *Journal of Philosophy* 66 (1969); 764–73. Both papers are reprinted in my *Reason and Teaching* (London: Routledge & Kegan Paul, 1973).

17. See the following selection in this volume.

18. See I. Scheffler, *Four Pragmatists* (London: Routledge and Kegan Paul, 1974), pp. 221–26 and 236–39.

14

Pragmatism as a Philosophy

Introduction

Pragmatism is popularly taken to be simply an attitude or a style, an emphasis on the practical or the social to the detriment of theoretical reflection and individual values. There are natural causes for such a construal, aside from the mere connotation of the word itself in everyday use. For pragmatic thinkers do in fact lay great stress upon practice, emphasizing the role of action in human thought, from the humblest bit of learning by a child exploring its room, to the most refined learning of the scientist manipulating the environment experimentally in order to explore the universe. Pragmatists, moreover, stress the social import of thinking—the structure of science as a community of investigators, the influence of historical contexts on the course of philosophy, and the relevance of philosophical inquiry to the problems of men.

Nevertheless, the popular conception of pragmatism is extremely misleading, untrue to the movement as a whole and to the works of its individual thinkers. For while it accurately reflects pragmatic emphases on action and society, it neglects to represent such emphases as arising out of philosophical inquiry, failing utterly to register the source of such inquiry in a struggle with abstract questions and issues. Seeing pragmatism simply as an emphasis, it ignores pragmatic efforts to formulate philosophical accounts of meaning and thought, truth and knowledge, reality and value.

No investigation of such efforts can avoid the conclusion that pragmatism is a serious philosophy, with deep roots in the philosophical tradition. With the exception of William James, whose thought derived from British empiricism, the Cambridge pragmatists were indeed, as Murphey has called them, Kant's children,[1] and the movement as a whole may be largely interpreted

---

I have drawn upon the treatment in my *Four Pragmatists* (London: Routledge & Kegan Paul, 1974), for various aspects of the present paper. The paper appeared in K. Oehler, ed., *Zeichen und Realität* (Tübingen: Stauffenburg Verlag, 1984).

as an extension of Kantian themes into the scientific and social worlds of the nineteenth century. Charles Sanders Peirce, who took the very name "pragmatism" from Kant, was steeped in the history of philosophy and developed his thinking through interaction with the great philosophical masters of the past as well as the science and mathematics of his own day. Rejecting Cartesianism, he formulated challenging new conceptions of meaning and reality through reflection on the methods of the natural sciences, and strove all his life to develop a complete system of philosophy, in the spirit of the Kantian architectonic.

William James, a sensitive psychologist as well as a bold philosophical thinker, sought not only to advance the empirical study of mental phenomena but also to develop an adequate metaphysical interpretation of such phenomena and of the main features of human life as known to us by whatever source. He sought a view that would, in particular, do justice to individual freedom, to the reality of human choice, and to the stubbornness and disjointedness of particular facts as against what he called the "block universe" of Idealism. George Herbert Mead, philosopher and social psychologist, worked out a developmental approach to the mind-body problem, in which the central role was played by symbolism. Starting from Wilhelm Wundt's theory of gesture as communication of meaning, Mead elaborated a radical view of mind and self, as well as language, as emerging out of society, rather than the reverse. His study of symbolism yielded rich and suggestive interpretations of communication, conscience, and human community. Finally, John Dewey, who began his thinking career as a Hegelian, retained forever after characteristic marks of his Hegelian beginnings: a pronounced developmentalism, a respect for the force of ideas and, above all, an urge to unify opposites—to achieve a vision of the inclusive whole within which particular doctrines in conflict may be seen to represent but partial accounts of reality.

These pragmatist thinkers were intellectually and spiritually very different. Peirce's inspiration was the logic of science; his vision was of the ideal and the general: the ideal community of investigators, the general purport of ideas, the long-run approximation to reality through the self-corrective method of science. James's inspiration was rather the individual life of the individual creature, the predicaments of personal choice, the open options defining the particular act, the flow of time and mind, the religious perspective of the single human agent. Mead's vision was, further, social and evolutionary, his effort to understand the distinctive features of human community, as made possible through the growth of symbolic function. And Dewey's aim was in the broadest sense practical and moral, to reconstruct human arrangements through fostering the habit of intelligence—making reflection practical and practice reflective by relating both thought and action to their anticipated meanings in experience.

Although different in their several primary concerns and emphases, these pragmatic thinkers nevertheless joined in producing a distinctive philosophical orientation, rooted in the intellectual past but responsive to the intellectual challenges of the present. They sought indeed to bring philosophical conceptions up-to-date through analysis of the new science and its methods, while placing science itself within a philosophical framework featuring a new approach to meaning. And they sought further to apply their philosophical conceptions in understanding the unprecedented circumstances and the challenges facing human society in the modern world.

The nineteenth-century world in which pragmatism developed was a world in which important oppositions were at work: science versus religion, positivism versus romanticism, intuition versus sense experience. The characteristic posture of pragmatism in response to such oppositions was that of a mediating philosophy, attempting to bridge science and religion, theory and practice, fact and value, speculative thought and analysis, tender-minded and tough-minded temperaments (as James put it), and (with Dewey) school and life. This mediating posture differentiates pragmatism from other philosophical tendencies inspired by science. In particular, pragmatism contrasts with positivism in refusing to assimilate intellectual interests generally to some simplified model of positive science. Responsive in particular to evolutionary thought and the new statistical modes of inference, pragmatism was indeed led to revise inherited conceptions of science itself. And, rather than using science as a device for dismissing or downgrading other modes of experience, such as art, history, morality, religion, philosophy, and social practice, pragmatism has taken science primarily as exemplifying general concepts of critical thought, in terms of which important continuities among all the modes might be revealed, and in light of which they might all be refined and brought to bear intelligently upon human problems.

I. Problems of Pragmatism and Pragmatic Responses

Pragmatism developed in a period of enormous social and intellectual change—a time that Max Fisch has named the "classical period" in America, from the end of the Civil War to the eve of the Second World War.[2] Dewey's life spanned this period, and Gail Kennedy has described its course as follows:

> He was born on the eve of the great war that was to ensure the triumph in America of industrialism and economic enterprise, in the year that Darwin published his *Origin of Species,* the book which marked the coming of age of modern science. He grew up in the environment of the older America, in the Vermont town of Burlington. Here life was still

largely unaffected by the newer science and by modern industrialism. From this small community with its simple and intimate round of handicraft and agricultural occupations, the form of society that Jefferson knew, he was to go out into the complex world created by modern science and mass-production industries, to the first American university, the newly founded Johns Hopkins, to the fermenting democracy of the Middle West, in his years of teaching at the Universities of Michigan and Minnesota, then to the great industrial and commercial cities of Chicago and New York. Dewey has said in an autobiographical essay that the forces which influenced him came "from persons and from situations" rather than from books. It was the transition from the America of his boyhood to the new America of his maturity that created the basic problems and formed the central theme of his philosophy.[3]

This period of transition brought with it major intellectual, and not merely social, changes. Not only was there a challenge in science to traditional religion and morality; there was also a challenge to inherited conceptions of science and classical views of knowledge. The most important influence was that of evolution, promoting the biologizing of human intelligence and the continuity between mankind's capacities and those of the lower animals. The rise of experimental and historical sciences of man, as well, reinforced evolutionary ideas of process and continuity, and also brought out the adaptive variability in human custom. The new prominence of probabilistic and statistical concepts both in physics and biology required a revision of older conceptions of logic and science. Finally, while great social changes were complicating life, making liberty and choice more precarious, the new human sciences painted a more flexible picture to replace older notions of cultural fixity; the idea of a *social* science indeed held out the prospect of bringing tradition itself under a measure of control. Knowledge, it seemed, had now to be reconceived: arising out of a biological matrix, continuous with adaptive action addressed to environmental problems, it yielded provisional solutions rather than necessary truths, promising increased social control but therefore imposing increased moral responsibility.[4]

The changes here noted were taken by pragmatism to pose the following broad philosophical problems. First, how is our contemporary theory of knowledge to assimilate the new scientific understanding of change, of process, of biological and social factors, of probable reasoning? Classical rationalism and classical empiricism seemed both inadequate to the task, the one taking knowing as the work of the individual mind drawing up eternal truths from within, the other as the mind's passively registering ideas stamped on it from without.

Second, and more generally, how are we to articulate the new emphasis on *continuity,* connecting man's life with the world of nature, relating his knowledge and his values, his cognitions with his feelings and actions, his life as an intellect with his career as an organism in a particular biological and evolutionary setting? The basic problem, for pragmatism, was to find a way of overcoming inherited dualisms of knower and known, mind and body, fact and value, theory and practice, ends and means.

Third, how are we to find new sources of stability in the face of radical changes in scientific belief and—more urgently still—how to find sources of stability consonant with the experimental habit of mind underlying science? Rejecting what Dewey called "the quest for certainty" and adopting instead Peirce's attitude of "fallibilism," how could sufficient stability yet be found to sustain the arts of inquiry, of education, of culture, and the public life?

Fourth, how are we to conceive the prospects of individual selfhood and democratic community under the new conditions of industrial society? How can policy formation be institutionalized in today's circumstances so as to be responsive to those whom policy affects? How can technological advance be reconciled with humane purpose, with the values of the arts and of associated life, and with the primacy of critical intelligence as the chief ideal of education?

The pragmatists' response to these problems cannot be recounted here in any detail, but its main features may be related, in outline, to a single starting point, namely, the rejection of Cartesian philosophy. Rejecting the mind-body dualism of Descartes, pragmatism is, first of all, led to develop a *functional view of thought,* relating cognition to the purposive life of the organism, responding to problems set by its environment. Second, giving up Cartesian certainty, pragmatism proposes instead a *fallibilistic view of knowledge* as a provisional scheme of hypotheses, resting upon probable reasoning and pointed toward the future, remaining ever subject to the test of further experience. Third, surrendering Cartesian individualism, pragmatists offer in its place a *social conception of science* as the effort, not of single inquirers, but of an open-ended community of investigators to learn from experience in a systematic way. Finally, giving up Cartesian intuition, pragmatists alternatively propose the *representative character of thinking,* holding thought to be always and throughout symbolic, channeled through networks of interdependent sign processes, thus incapable of ever yielding either fixity or certainty. Symbolism enables thought to frame ends-in-view independent of actual outcomes, and so to anticipate and regulate conduct. Thus, writes Dewey, "The invention or discovery of symbols is doubtless by far the single greatest event in the history of man." Signs or symbols themselves are not *images or pictures* of reality; they are rather to be interpreted as devices of the purposeful life. "What now is a *conception?*" asks William James, and he answers: "It is a *teleological instrument.* It is a partial aspect of a thing which *for our purpose* we regard as its essential aspect, as the representative of the entire thing." "Wherever intelligence operates," writes Dewey, "things are judged in their capacity of signs of other things. If scientific knowledge enables us to estimate more accurately the worth of things as signs, we can afford to exchange a loss of theoretical certitude for a gain in practical judgment. For if we can judge events as indications of other events, we can prepare in all cases for the coming of what is anticipated," and take part as knowers in the purposive "direction of change."[5]

The consequences of these anti-Cartesian positions are far-reaching. Once certainty and individualism are surrendered as epistemic ideals and science reinterpreted as the continuous learning effort of an ideal community, stability is to be sought in the *intellectual method* defining such community. The conclusions of particular inquiries are indeed all provisional; they are probable at best and subject to revision by further investigation. But despite recurrent revisions of scientific doctrine, the community dedicated to systematic learning from experience is itself a continuous entity, unified by its allegiance to critical method. It is such allegiance that gives us ground to stand on even as we alter particular items of belief. The very self-correctiveness of science which forces the revision of its theories when they fall out of accord with the evidence constitutes a steady ideal standing firm throughout change. And while we cannot hope to be sure of any of our particular theories, we can be sure that the method of science will yield increasingly adequate theories through continued inquiry by the investigative community of mankind.

This investigative community offers, finally, a suggestive model for conceiving democratic society generally. As science institutionalizes procedures for investigating hypotheses about nature, so democratic society institutionalizes procedures for the critical testing of social ideas, plans, and policies— all to be conceived as hypothetical. Provisional agreements on particulars, whether in scientific research or in social action, are necessary and, indeed, sufficient to organize further collaborative efforts, but all particular ideas remain subject to the continuing test of experience, to be revised when necessary, in accord with the underlying unity of method.

In science, the open communication of ideas and their availability for testing by rival theorists is an essential point of method. In democratic society, too, an essential need is to ensure free communication among persons, so that their special perspectives may be appreciated by others and made available, moreover, for the general testing of social arrangements. Dewey's notion of *shared experience* does not refer to the having of the same experiences by all, but rather to the communication of diverse experiences by means of shared symbolic structures. The social problem is to develop and sustain such structures and, moreover, to facilitate their proper use. This requires breaking down artificial barriers to sympathetic communication and educating individuals for those skills and traits of character peculiarly consonant with democratic institutions. Of all the freedoms required by such institutions, freedom of mind is basic, for, without it, individuals are not genuinely free do develop. "Freed intelligence," says Dewey, "is necessary to direct and to warrant freedom of action."[6] It is the cultivation of free, sympathetic, and critical intelligence that constitutes at once the fundamental imperative of democracy and the main task of its education.

The foregoing sketch of pragmatic ideas provides at best a general and composite picture rather than an individual portrait of any single pragmatist. I shall therefore devote the remainder of my remarks to the pioneering work of Charles Sanders Peirce, the founder of the movement, focusing, in particular, upon his rejection of Descartes and the development of his influential alternative theory of belief, doubt, and inquiry.

II. Peirce's Theory of Belief, Doubt, and Inquiry

In place of Descartes's emphasis on *radical doubt* and Locke's emphasis on *sensations*, Peirce emphasizes *belief,* indeed placing the notion of belief at the center of his theory of inquiry. Thought, or inquiry, arises always in a context of belief, and it is precipitated by doubt. Doubt is, however, not the mere lack of belief; it is an active state of irritation, focused and specific rather than wholesale and diffuse like the Cartesian variety. Provoked by such irritation, inquiry arises, inquiry being the active process of passing from doubt to belief. Unlike doubt, belief is itself a calm, settled state of readiness, in the nature of a habit; it is not an episode or occurrence but more like a disposition or set. In Alexander Bain's words, it is that upon which we are prepared to act. Orienting us thus to future experience, belief is always, in consequence, open to upset by experience. Certainty of belief is therefore precluded. Indeed, since belief is expressible only in signs, with implicit reference to other signs, it is always mediated and never direct, hence in principle incapable of certainty. "From the proposition that every thought is a sign," says Peirce, "it follows that every thought must address itself to some other, must determine some other, since that is the essence of a sign."[7] All thoughts are thus in the same boat, all fallible, all interdependent. In place of Cartesian certainty, Peirce in fact espouses rather what he calls *fallibilism.*

The underpinnings of these ideas are developed in two papers of 1868, both devoted to criticism of Descartes. In the first of these, "Questions Concerning Certain Faculties Claimed for Man," Peirce criticizes the doctrine of intuition or immediate knowledge. In the second, "Some Consequences of Four Incapacities," he concentrates on issues of logic and methodology. "We cannot," he says in the latter paper, "begin with complete doubt," since doubt requires a positive reason. Even in philosophy, this principle ought to hold. "Let us not pretend to doubt in philosophy what we do not doubt in our hearts."[8] Radical Cartesian doubt, since it is in fact impossible, must be empty and self-deceptive. Its impotence is revealed by the fact that the Cartesian method that begins with radical doubt ends by recovering all the beliefs with which the doubter began. Real doubt, on the other hand, as illustrated by a typical research question in the sciences, is focused and motivated, framed by a variety of assumptions meanwhile taken for granted. Such doubt is not impotent; it has, indeed, the power to stimulate inquiry that may in the end alter the beliefs of the doubter. Each provisional assumption may, furthermore, be doubted in its turn, but at no time are *all* assumptions thrown into doubt at once.

Peirce considered Alexander Bain's definition of belief as "that upon which a man is prepared to act" as the basis of his pragmatism.[9] Bain's view, as Murphey suggests, supplied the "psychological foundation for Peirce's denial of Cartesian doubt, for Bain holds that men are naturally believers and that doubt is produced only by events which disrupt our beliefs—not by pretense."[10] Rather than supposing that the "natural" state is utter lack of belief, i.e., *radical doubt,* so that every belief we have requires justification from scratch, Bain offers Peirce a theory that reverses the order of natural-ness, as the modern concept of inertia reversed the natural state from rest to motion. The natural psychological state is now held to be that of belief, with no possibility of wholesale and radical justification. Rather, doubt arising in the body of our beliefs now wants a positive reason, and it finds resolution in the recapture of belief. Using Bain's idea, Peirce can, as Murphey points out,

> fit his whole theory of inquiry into an evolutionary frame of reference. Beliefs may be regarded as adjustive habits while failure of adjustment leads to doubt. . . . This biological perspective . . . provides him with a new definition of the nature of a problem—a definition subsequently developed by Dewey. A problem situation exists whenever we find our established habits of conduct inadequate to attain a desired end, . . . and the effect of a problem situation upon us is the production of doubt. This being the case, Cartesian doubt is nonsense, for there is no problem situation. But secondly, the theory provides a clarification of the nature of an answer. An answer is any rule of action which enables us to attain our desired ends. Accordingly, our objective is to find a rule which will always lead us to that which we desire. So in the investigation of a real object, our objective is a knowledge of how to act respecting that object so as to attain our desired ends. Thus, as pragmatism asserts, the concept of the object can mean nothing to us but all the habits it involves. The attainment of a stable belief—belief that will stand in the long run—is thus the goal of inquiry. Such belief we define as true, and its objects as reality.[11]

In his 1877 paper "The Fixation of Belief," Peirce presents a full statement of his theory. Doubt differs from belief in three respects, he says. First, "there is a dissimilarity between the sensation of doubting and that of believing";

second, "the feeling of believing is a more or less sure indication of there being established in our nature some habit which will determine our actions. Doubt never has such an effect"; and third, "doubt is an uneasy and dissatisfied state from which we struggle to free outselves and pass into the state of belief, while the latter is a calm and satisfactory state which we do not wish to avoid, or to change to a belief in anything else. On the contrary, we cling tenaciously, not merely to believing, but to believing just what we do believe."[12]

Inquiry, now, is the struggle to overcome doubt and attain belief, and it has in doubt its "only immediate motive." It begins with doubt and ends only with the cessation of doubt. Therefore, says Peirce, "The sole object of inquiry is the settlement of opinion." When opinion is settled and "real and living doubt" overcome, genuine inquiry cannot arise. When no *actual* doubt affects any given proposition, it does not matter that it might *possibly* be thrown into doubt by hypothetical considerations.

III. Peirce's Comparison of Methods

If the function of inquiry is indeed the settlement of opinion, or the fixation of belief, the question may be raised as to the relative effectiveness of alternative methods by which this function may be carried out. Considering this question, Peirce proceeds to a comparison of four such methods: the method of tenacity, the method of authority, the a priori method, and the method of science. Simple tenacity, i.e., a reiteration of the belief, "dwelling on all which may conduce to that belief, and learning to turn with contempt and hatred from anything which might disturb it" is a method "really pursued by many men" and offering "great peace of mind" despite some inconveniences. But it is ineffective for, as Peirce says, "the social impulse is against it." Finding oneself confronted with the differing opinions of others, one's confidence in one's own tenaciously held beliefs is shaken. Nor can we shield ourselves from contacts with others unless we become hermits. Tenacity thus leaves us vulnerable to continual unsettlement of our beliefs.

The method of authority, tranferring tenacity to the group, utilizes social or political institutions to inculcate preferred doctrines and to stamp out contrary views. A whole array of repressive measures is available, e.g., censorship, indoctrination, terror, with occasional massacres as needed for, as Peirce remarks, these have proved "very effective means of settling opinion in a country." The method of authority is capable of atrocity for, says Peirce, "the officer of a society does not feel justified in surrendering the interests of that society for the sake of mercy, as he might his own private interests." As to effectiveness, authority is superior to tenacity, shielding the individual, by and large, from encounters with differing opinions. But is has its own sources of inefficiency nevertheless: social regulation cannot extend to all opinions whatever, and unregulated opinion always poses a potential threat to settled belief. Individuals may reflect that other societies and other ages have held quite different beliefs, and conclude that it is mere historical accident that has led them to the official doctrines they have. Such doubts must, says Peirce, affect "every belief which seems to be determined by the caprice either of themselves or of those who originated the popular opinions."

The a priori method rejects tenacity as well as the effort to force one's beliefs on others. Rather, it follows the natural preferences of "men conversing together and regarding matters in different lights." The chief example of the operation of this method is to be found in "the history of metaphysical philosophy," where beliefs have been formed not in the effort to account for observed facts but rather in the effort to formulate what seemed "agreeable to reason." Enjoying greater intellectual respectability than either of the others already considered, this method nevertheless fails equally. It is ineffective since it assimilates inquiry to the development of taste, always a matter of fashion, and thus never culminates in agreement but remains always subject to pendulum swings over time. When we reflect on the diversity of fashion, we recognize our own beliefs to have been formed by such "accidental causes," and new doubts arise again to unsettle these beliefs.

The method of science, finally, is one that purports to form beliefs by reference to external permanencies rather than human causes. It supposes real things with properties "entirely independent of our opinions about them." It is true, says Peirce, that the supposition of realities cannot be proved by science, since it *underlies* science, but practice of the scientific method never leads us to doubt this supposition, whereas practice of the other methods does lead us to doubt them. To question the existence of real things *in general* is idle: "If there be anybody with a living doubt upon the subject," says Peirce, "let him consider it." But the fundamental contrast between the method of science and all the others is that it is the only one that presents "any distinction of a right and a wrong way." The method, that is to say, is self-corrective, acknowledging the possibility of errors in application corrigible by further use of the method itself. By contrast, the result of applying any of the other methods is necessarily correct according to the method in question, so that no errors can be admitted, much less corrected, by the method itself. While the other methods have their virtues, a man should reflect, says Peirce, that "after all, he wishes his opinions to coincide with the fact, and that there is no reason why the results of those first three methods should do so. To bring about this effect is the prerogative of the method of science."

IV. Difficulties in Peirce's Treatment

The doubt-belief theory of inquiry is central to Peirce's general conceptions of mind, meaning, truth, and reality. It appealed to him in the first instance as providing a psychological foundation for his epistemological critique of Descartes. Read purely as psychology, it seems to me, however, obscure on several points, which I have elaborated more fully in my book *Four Pragmatists*. For example, is doubt always conscious or may it simply be inferred from its characteristic disruptive effects on conduct? Although described as an occurrent state of irritation, it might still theoretically be construed as not implying consciousness in every case; yet Peirce affirms a "sensation of doubting." Does he then call the characteristic disruptive effects minus the characteristic sensation "doubt" or not? The answer is unclear.

To take another example, how, if belief is a habit or set, can Peirce speak of a "sensation of believing" and describe it (in the companion essay "How to Make Our Ideas Clear") as "something we are aware of"? More important, how can he say of belief (in this same essay) that it "appeases the irritation of doubt," having earlier argued that belief is prior to doubt, constituting indeed the natural state of the mind before inquiry. Finally, what does Peirce intend in saying that belief involves the establishment of a rule of action or a habit? Since not all habits are associated with beliefs, does he have any way of specifying which subclass of habits is peculiarly belief-related? Does he, similarly, have any way of indicating which disruptions of conduct are constitutive of doubt? To me, at any rate, these unanswered questions indicate basic obscurities in the theory, under a psychological interpretation.

However, the theory may be given an *epistemological* rather than a *psychological* interpretation; taken thus, it is not necessarily vulnerable to the difficulties just outlined, and it requires a fresh evaluation. Interpreted epistemologically, the theory purports not to *describe* but rather to *prescribe* the course of thought, construed as a critical or scientific effort. Properly, the theory declares, such thought always addresses specific questions arising from real doubt, proceeding in every case by taking a variety of assumptions for granted throughout the inquiry, and subject to evaluation by seeing how well it turns out to resolve the questions from which it arose. The theory thus rejects the idea that there can be scientific investigations without assumptions altogether, and it equally rejects the idea that assumptions actually adopted must be absolutely indubitable.

Although this epistemological version of the theory does indeed escape the problems of the psychological reading, Peirce's insistence on "real and living doubt" as the proper origin of inquiry still poses a difficulty. For there is, in fact, much thinking of a significant kind that does not originate in doubt. Imagination, recollection, perception, translation, composition—all seem to provide counterinstances. In reply, it will be said that Peirce is concerned, not with thinking in general, but with *inquiry* specifically, in particular as exemplified in scientific research. Is it then the case that all such research originates, or should originate, in real and living doubt? Does there really need to be an active irritation, a breakdown in earlier habits, before scientific research can be initiated? Does not theoretical curiosity have a role in the stimulation of inquiry? Peirce insists, to the contrary, that genuine thought arises from real and active irritation rather than from theoretical or speculative motives.

Nevertheless, he displays increasing ambivalence on this central point. As early as 1878, in "How to Make Our Ideas Clear," he speaks of "feigned hesitancy," saying that "whether feigned for mere amusement or with a lofty purpose," it "plays a great part in the production of scientific inquiry."[13] Then, in a note added in 1893 to "The Fixation of Belief," he states that doubt is typically "anticipated hesitancy about what I shall do hereafter, or a feigned hesitancy about a fictitious state of things. It is the power of making believe we hesitate, together with the pregnant fact that the decision upon the merely make-believe dilemma goes toward forming a bona fide habit that will be operative in a real emergency."[14] Finally, in a note of 1903, he says tnat "for the sake of the pleasures of inquiry, men may like to seek out doubts."[15] The net effect of these qualifications is surely to deny that research must always spring from actual difficulties, real irritations, or living doubts; it is also to acknowledge that the researcher is motivated not only to solve problems but to seek them. Research activity, in sum, does not subside when real doubts are dispelled, real problems resolved—for the generation of feigned doubts and hypothetical problems continues unabated.

Peirce's theory of inquiry, even under epistemological interpretation, thus remains difficult. In its unqualified form, it clashes with the fact of theoretical motivation in research. Taken together with its supplementary qualifications, it appears inconsistent. The qualified theory, moreover, undercuts Peirce's earlier criticism of Descartes. For, having himself insisted on the role of feigned or hypothetical doubt in science, how can Peirce dismiss Descartes's radical doubt as mere idle pretense?

V. An Epistemological Interpretation

My own view is that Peirce's formulation, *that all inquiry must begin in real and living doubt,* is indeed untenable. It implies that without real and living doubt there can be no inquiry; yet Peirce admits the importance of inquiries springing from doubts that are merely feigned. Once feigned inquiries are admitted, however, what differentiates Peirce's notion of doubt from the radical doubt of Descartes? What is the distinctive import of Peirce's theory?

I suggest the answer lies in the *role* ascribed to feigned doubt. For Descartes's method, feigned doubt disqualifies a proposition from serving as an assumption, since what he seeks are assumptions not only undoubted but indubitable. For Peirce, on the other hand, a proposition that is as a matter of fact undoubted, i.e., free of real and living doubt, still qualifies as an assumption, even though subject to feigned doubt. The mere fact that one might *hypothetically* doubt such a proposition does not *require* us to reject it as an assumption and try to replace it, or perhaps reinstate it through additional argumentation. We are *required* to disqualify assumptions only if they are subject to real and living doubts—that is, doubts that are specific to the propositions in question and that rest on positive reasons. But a proposition we are are not *required* to reject as an assumption may be rejected anyhow for the space of a given hypothetical inquiry, during which other undoubted assumptions are meanwhile retained. Inquiries may, in other words, indeed originate in feigned doubt; such feigning is consistent with use of the proposition in question as an assumption in other inquiries; the mere possibility of such feigning does not render assumptions generally useless.

Peirce, according to this interpretation, is here rejecting the unconditional or wholesale doubt of radical scepticism, insisting that inquiry may stand on undoubted although dubitable assumptions, even as it proceeds to investigate others taken as problematic. The sceptic, doubting all assumptions short of indubitability, leaves himself no room to stand and allows himself no resources for dealing with the problems he raises. He errs, not in his feigning as such, but in his demand that all hypothetically dubitable propositions be simultaneously feigned to be useless as assumptions. By contrast, scientific doubt, whether it is real or feigned, is always specific, resting on provisional assumptions that serve usefully as premises of the inquiry even though they fall short of absolute certainty. Nor is the scientific researcher's work done when his problem is solved, for he will then try to find, imagine, or construct new problems specific enough to be formulable as testable questions. The answer to the sceptical yearning for certainty at the outset thus lies in the continuity of fallible inquiries tending toward the fixation of beliefs in the future.

VI. The Primacy of Method

Consider now Peirce's comparison of methods in "The Fixation of Belief," a comparison that is very puzzling indeed. For Peirce promises to compare his four methods solely by reference to their relative effectiveness in stabilizing belief since, as he says, "the settlement of opinion is the sole object of inquiry." Yet, in defending the method of science, he does not even mention its superior effectiveness, but invokes instead a variety of new considerations, some metaphysical (relating to the supposition of real things), some methodological (relating to self-correctiveness), some epistemological (relating to the need for opinions to aspire to coincidence with fact), and some even moral ("to avoid looking into the support of any belief from a fear that it may turn out rotten is quite as immoral as it is disadvantageous").

Moreover, to defend science as more successful than the other methods in settling belief seems doomed to failure anyhow. Science does not, like the method of tenacity, yield "great peace of mind." Indeed the rate of change of scientific opinions would seem to be higher than that associated with any of the other methods. What is characteristic of science is that it places all its claims in perpetual jeopardy, making them forever vulnerable to unsettlement. It might perhaps be thought plausible to defend scientific method through appeal to the restless spirit of man, relishing the prospect of a continued unfixing of beliefs and recasting of received doctrines. How could Peirce have hoped to succeed in the exactly opposite course?

Perhaps, it might be said, the mere *change* of scientific opinion is not fatal to the notion of science as stabilizing belief. For such change may be construed as uniformly *progressive,* i.e., as adding to reliable information without disturbing the already available stock, as sharpening the vaguer formulations of the past, or as steadily narrowing the range of opinion in a process of approximation to an ideal limit. Such a conception is reflected in the important passage in "How to Make Our Ideas Clear" in which Peirce says that truth is "the opinion which is fated to be ultimately agreed to by all who investigate . . . , and the object represented in this opinion is the real." Scientists, he says, "may at first obtain different results, but, as each perfects his method and his processes, the results will move steadily together toward a destined center."[16]

This idea is, however, vulnerable to two criticisms. First, the concept of approximation may be suitable for measurements, but it does not fit theories. As Quine has remarked, "the notion of limit depends on that of 'nearer than,' which is defined for numbers and not for theories."[17] Second, science does not simply add information or sharpen vague formulations or steadily converge in opinion; it often changes theoretical direction and rejects previous beliefs. Even if experimental and technological knowledge *does* tend to accumulate, even if later theories, in accounting for a wider range of such knowledge, are considered not merely *different from* but *superior to* earlier theories, still theoretical change must be recognized to be nonprogressive: the theoretical agreement of a given period is often uprooted and superseded by a *conflicting* agreement in a later period. And this is incompatible with the project of showing science to be maximally effective in *fixing beliefs in general.* It is perhaps, I conjecture, some such train of thought that accounts for the first difficulty with the essay, i.e., that the defense of the method of science shifts ground, moving from a consideration of effectiveness to other considerations of various sorts.

These latter considerations have this in common: they transfer attention from the stability of *particular beliefs* to that of *methods,* arguing that the method of science is *itself* firmer than the other methods discussed. Because it rests on the undoubted supposition of real things, because it is self-corrective, because it tests beliefs not by reference to human attitudes, intuitions, or institutions but rather by reference to those facts to which the beliefs purport to refer, scientific method is itself capable of standing firm through the change of specific beliefs. To challenge a particular belief sanctioned by any of the other methods calls the method itself into question because none of these methods is capable of allowing consistent correction of its own pronouncements. These methods are *brittle,* incapable of absorbing change without fracture. The method of science, by contrast, achieves stablility through flexibility. Rejecting pretensions to certainty, opening wide the testing process to all members of the ideal community of investigators, requiring continual correction to account for all available facts, the method is itself capable of absorbing change without upset.

Since, however, the essay thus shifts the question of stability from the level of belief to that of method, it does not in fact fulfill its promise. Yet the defence of science it offers is of interest in its own right, exemplifying, moreover, that emphasis on the primacy of method that is characteristic of pragmatic philosophy in all its variants. It is method rather than doctrine that defines the community of investigation, and it is the stability of method in pursuit of the truth that holds this community together throughout doctrinal change. Similarly, for pragmatic social theory, it is the method embodied in democratic institutions that defines the community dedicated to the qualities of human freedom and dignity, and it is the stability of democratic methods that may hold the community together through changes of policy and belief.

The task of education, finally, is to teach proper method. Its special function, as Dewey emphasized, is not to indoctrinate a particular point of view but rather to develop those powers of logical assessment and criticism by which diverse points of view may themselves be evaluated. Method, moreover, is the key to intellectual advance, and education therefore has another powerful motivation to stress method as primary. It is this aspect of education to which Peirce attaches the greatest importance. Construing logic as a methodical study of methods, and associating it with the general theory of signs, he writes: "When new paths have to be struck out, a spinal cord is not enough; a brain is needed, and that brain an organ of mind, and that mind perfected by a liberal education. And a liberal education—so far as its relation to the understanding goes—means *logic.*"[18]

Notes

1. Murray G. Murphey, "Kant's Children: The Cambridge Pragmatists," *Transactions of the Charles S. Peirce Society* 4, 3–33.

2. Max H. Fisch, *Classic American Philosophers* (New York: Appleton-Century-Crofts, 1951, 1966), preface and general introduction.

3. Gail Kennedy, "Introduction to John Dewey," in Fisch, *Classic American Philosophers,* pp. 328–29.

4. See Fisch, "The Classic Period in American Philosophy," in Fisch, *Classic American Philosophers,* pp. 10–12.

5. John Dewey, *The Quest for Certainty* (New York: Minton, Balch & Co., 1929), p. 151; William James, *Collected Essays and Reviews* (New York: Longmans, Green, 1920) pp. 86–87; quoted in Fisch, *Classic American Philosophers,* p. 26; and Dewey, *The Quest for Certainty,* p. 213.

6. John Dewey, "Democracy and Educational Administration," *School and Society* (1937): 457–62; reprinted in J. Ratner, *Intelligence in the Modern World* (New York: Modern Library, 1939), p. 404.

7. Peirce, "Questions Concerning Certain Faculties Claimed for Man," *Collected Papers,* 5.253.

8. Ibid., 5.265.

9. Ibid., 5.12–13.

10. Murray G. Murphey, *The Development of Peirce's Philosophy* (Cambridge, Mass.: Harvard University Press, 1961), p. 161.

11. Ibid., p. 163.

12. Peirce, *Collected Papers,* 5:370ff.

13. Ibid., 5.394.

14. Ibid., 5.373, n. 1.

15. Ibid., 5.372, n. 2.

16. Ibid., 5.407.

17. W. V. Quine, *Word and Object* (New York: Technology Press of M.I.T. and John Wiley, 1960), p. 23.

18. From the *Johns Hopkins University Circulars* (November 1882) as excerpted by M. H. Fisch and J. I. Cope, "Peirce at the Johns Hopkins University," in *Studies in the Philosophy of C. S. Peirce,* ed. Philip P. Wiener and Frederic H. Young (Cambridge, Mass.: Harvard University Press, 1952), pp. 289–90, reprinted in Wiener, *C. S. Peirce: Selected Writings* (New York: Dover, 1958), pp. 336–37.

Index